POP SONGS FOR KIDS

EASY PIANO

ISBN 978-1-4950-8961-9

HAL•LEONARD®

7777 W. BLUEMOUND RD. P.O. BOX 13819 MILWAUKEE, WI 53213

D1473558

Visit Hal Leonard Online at
www.halleonard.com

BACK TO DECEMBER

Words and Music by
TAYLOR SWIFT

1. I'm so glad you made time to see me. How's life?
2. *(See additional lyrics)*

Tell me, how's your fam - 'ly? I have - n't seen them in a

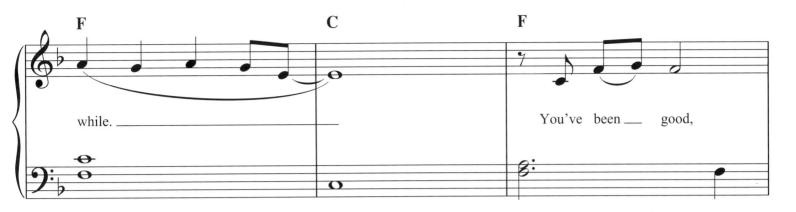

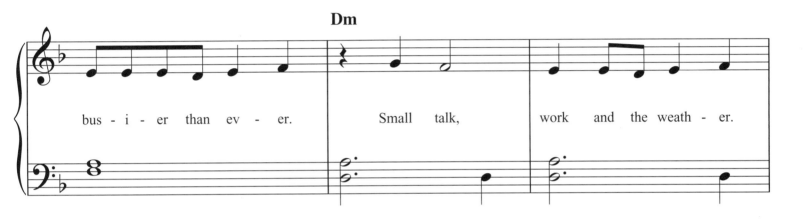

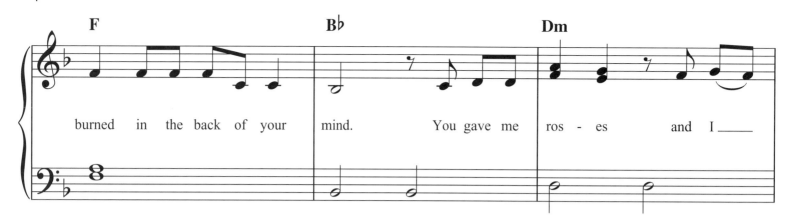

burned in the back of your mind. You gave me ros - es and I ____

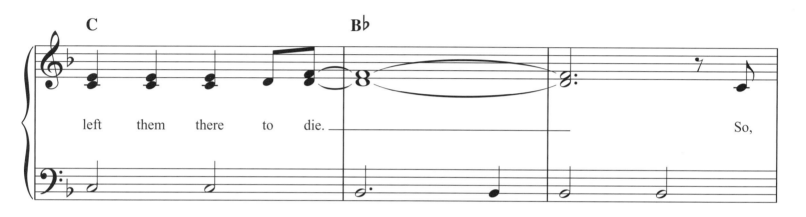

left them there to die. ____ So,

this is me swal - low - in' my pride stand - in' in front of you, say - in' I'm

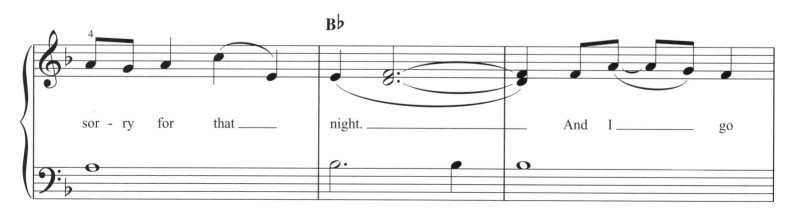

sor - ry for that ____ night. ____ And I ____ go

back to De - cem - ber all _____ the time. _ It turns out free - dom ain't

noth - in' but miss - in' you, wish - in' that I re - al - ized what I had ___ when

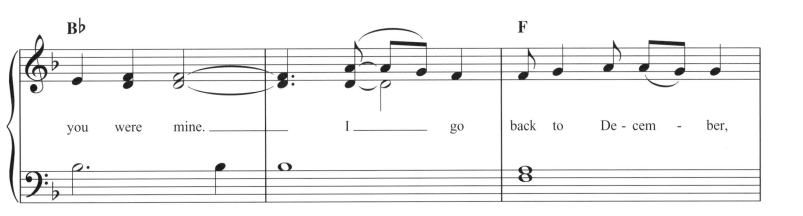

you were mine. _____ I _____ go back to De - cem - ber,

To Coda

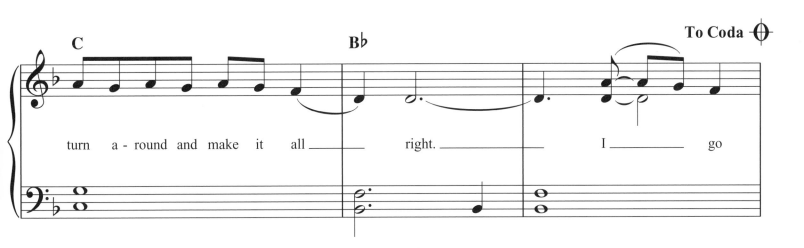

turn a - round and make it all ___ right. _____ I _____ go

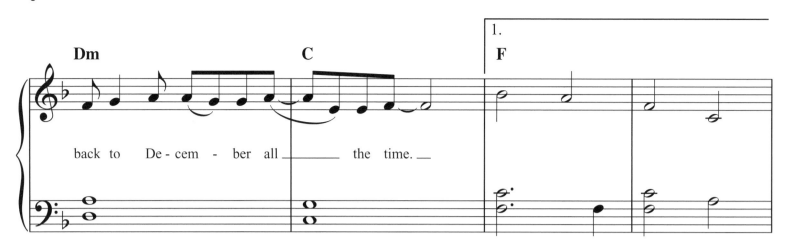

back to De - cem - ber all ____ the time. ____

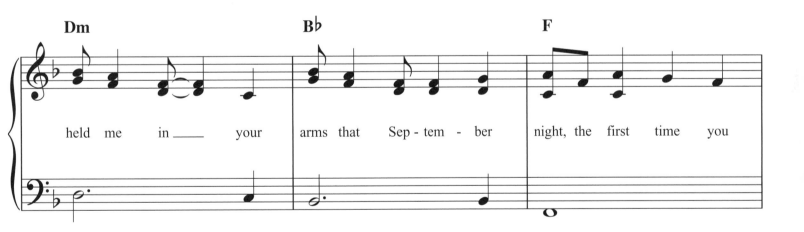

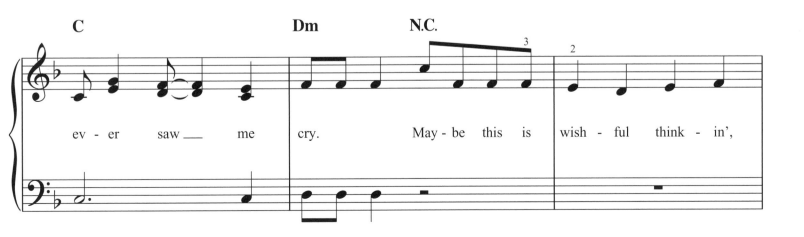

prob - a - bly   mind - less dream - in'.   If we loved a - gain,__

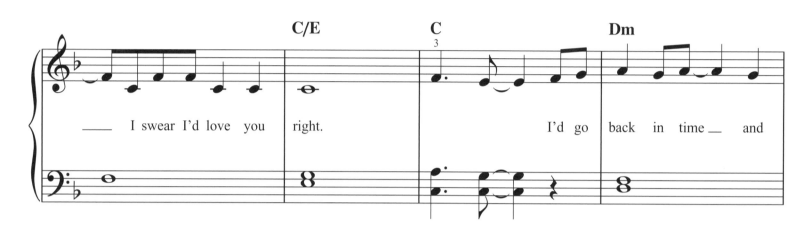

__ I swear I'd love you right.   I'd go back in time __ and

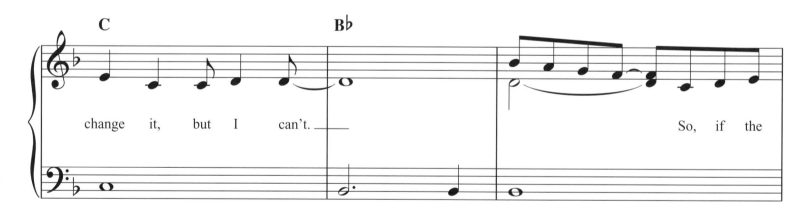

change it, but I can't.__   So, if the

D.S. al Coda

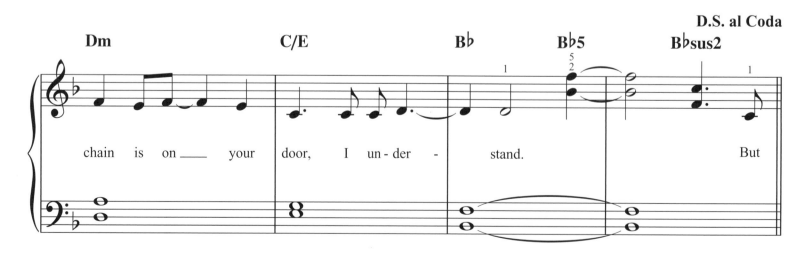

chain is on __ your door, I un - der -   stand.   But

back to De - cem - ber all _____ the time. __

poco rit.

Additional Lyrics

2. These days I haven't been sleepin';
    Stayin' up, playin' back myself leavin',
    When your birthday passed and I didn't call.
    Then I think about summer, all the beautiful times
    I watched you laughin' from the passenger side
    And realized I loved you in the fall.
    And then the cold came, the dark days
    When fear crept into my mind.
    You gave me all your love and
    All I gave you was goodbye.

    So, this is me swallowin' my pride...

BAD DAY

Words and Music by
DANIEL POWTER

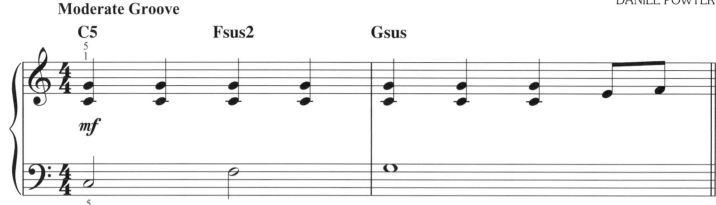

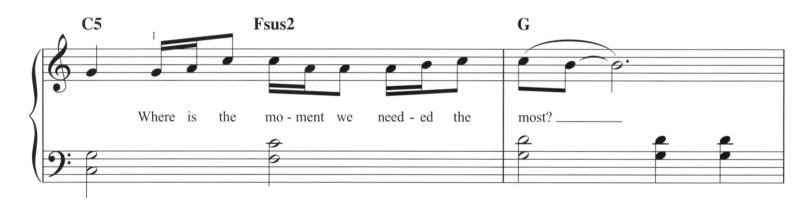

Where is the mo-ment we need-ed the most? ____

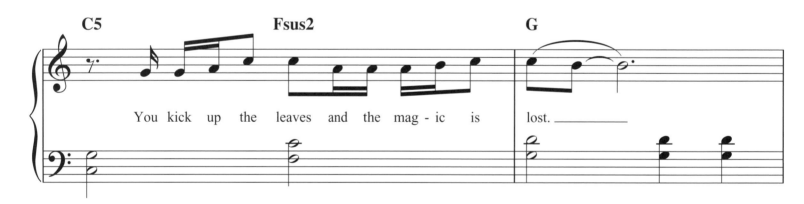

You kick up the leaves and the mag-ic is lost. ____

They tell me your blue skies fade to grey. They tell me your pas-sion's gone a-

way and I don't need no car-ryin' on.   You stand in the line just to hit a new

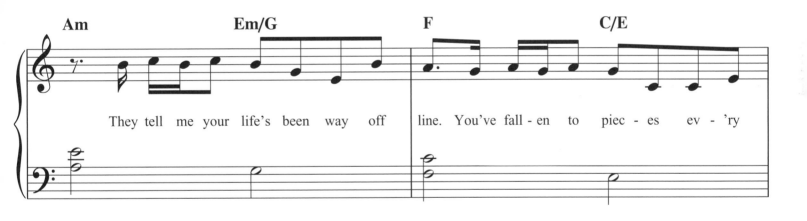

low. _____   You're fak-in' the smile with the cof-fee to   go. ___

They tell me your life's been way off   line. You've fall-en to piec-es ev-'ry

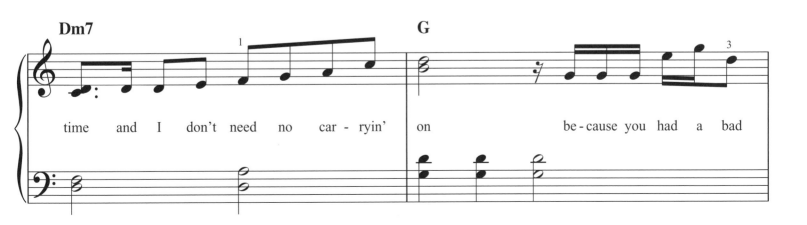

time and I don't need no car-ryin'   on   be-cause you had a bad

day. You're tak-in' one down. You sing a sad song just to turn it a-round. You say you don't

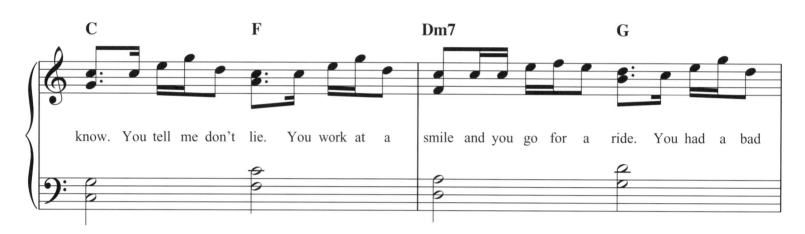

know. You tell me don't lie. You work at a smile and you go for a ride. You had a bad

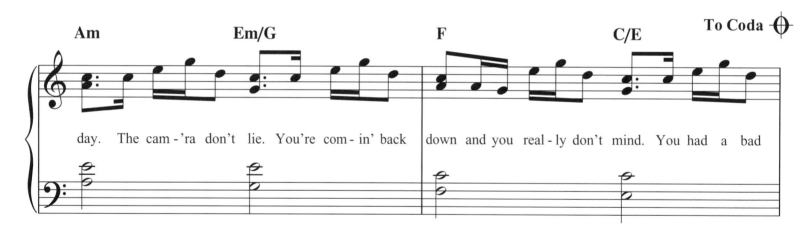

day. The cam-'ra don't lie. You're com-in' back down and you real-ly don't mind. You had a bad

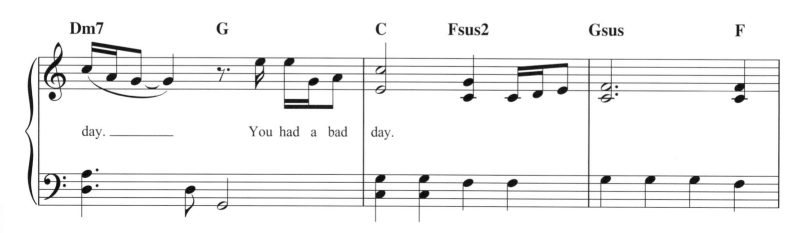

day. _____ You had a bad day.

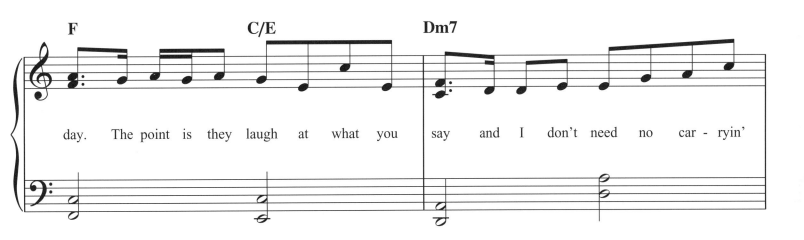

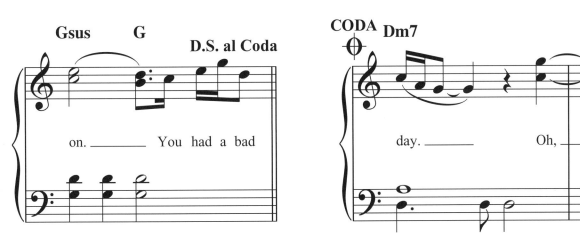

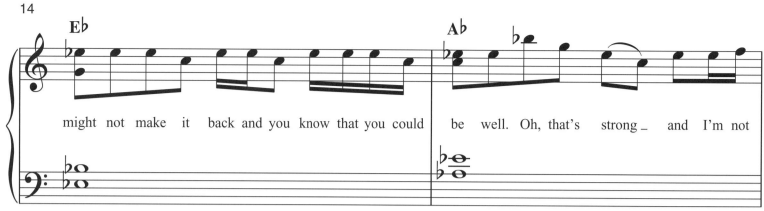

might not make it back and you know that you could be well. Oh, that's strong __ and I'm not

wrong, yeah. __ So where is the pas-sion when you need it the

most? __ Oh, you and I. You kick up the leaves and the mag - ic is

lost __ 'cause you had a bad day. You're tak - in one down. You sing a sad

song just to turn it a - round. You say you don't know. You tell me don't lie. You work at a

smile and you go for a ride. You had a bad day. You've seen what you like. And how does it

feel one more time? You had a bad day. _____ You had a bad day.

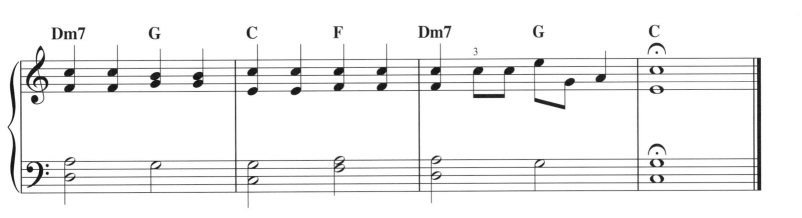

CAN'T STOP THE FEELING
from TROLLS

Words and Music by JUSTIN TIMBERLAKE,
MAX MARTIN and SHELLBACK

Moderate Funk groove

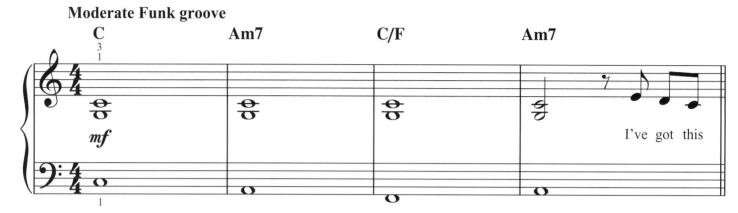

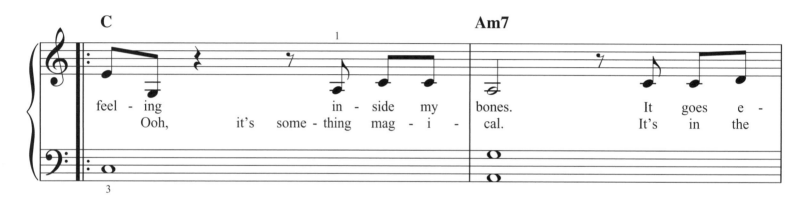

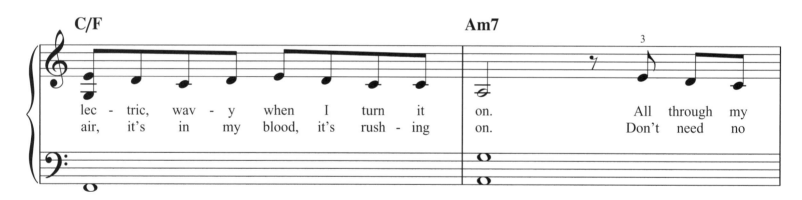

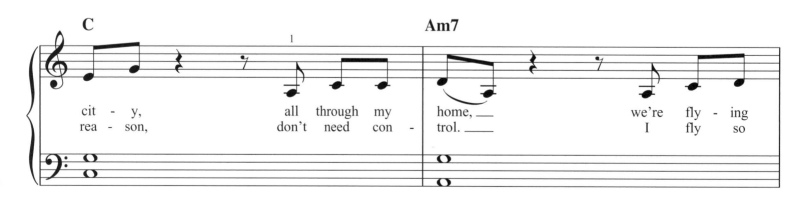

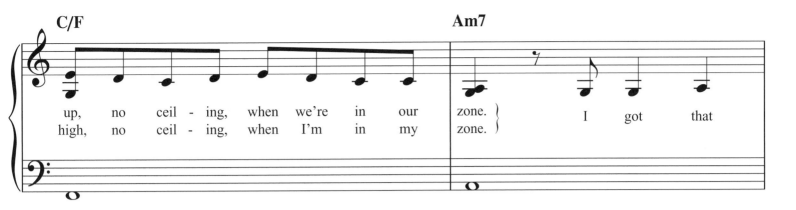

up, no ceil - ing, when we're in our zone.
high, no ceil - ing, when I'm in my zone.

I got that

sun-shine in my pock - et, got that good soul in my feet. I feel that hot blood in my bod - y when it

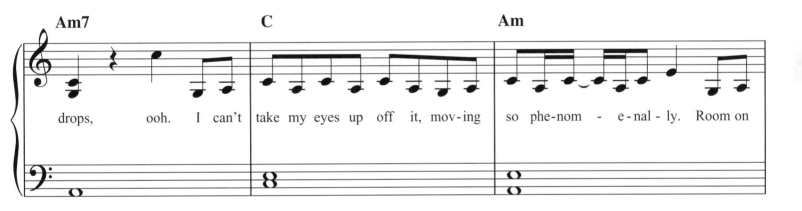

drops, ooh. I can't take my eyes up off it, mov-ing so phe-nom - e - nal - ly. Room on

lock the way we rock it, so don't stop. Un - der the lights when ev - 'ry-thing

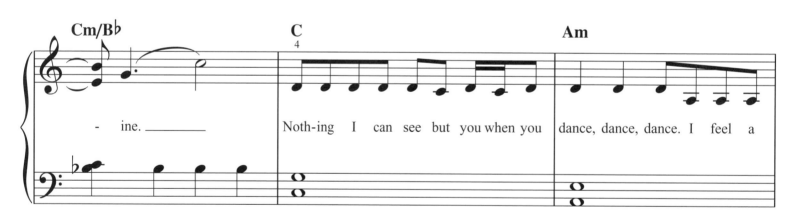

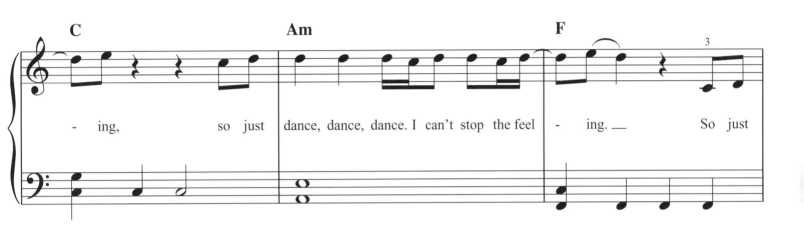

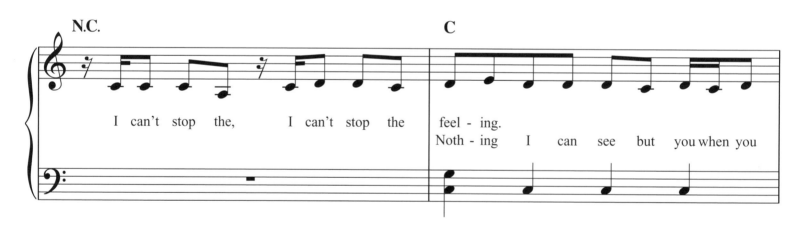

dance, dance, dance. Come on! All those things I should-n't do, but you

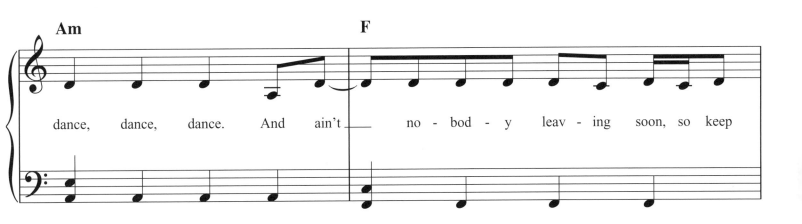

dance, dance, dance. And ain't no - bod - y leav - ing soon, so keep

danc - ing. I can't stop the feel - ing. Got this feel-ing in my

bod - y. I can't stop the feel - ing. Got this feel - ing in my

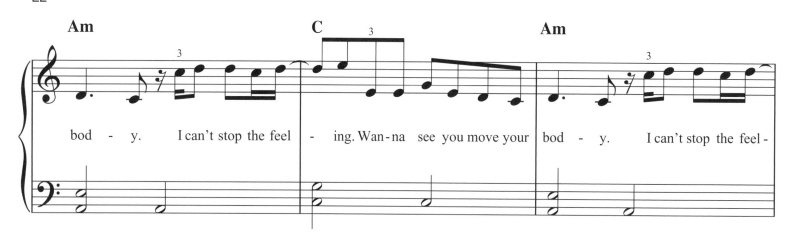

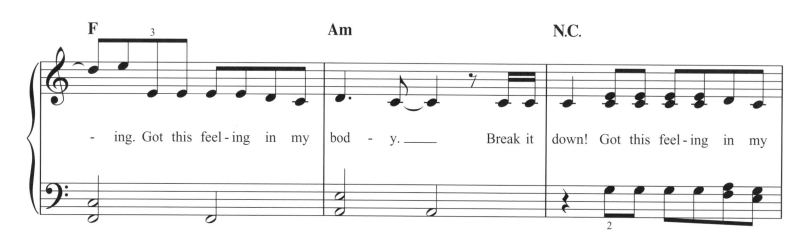

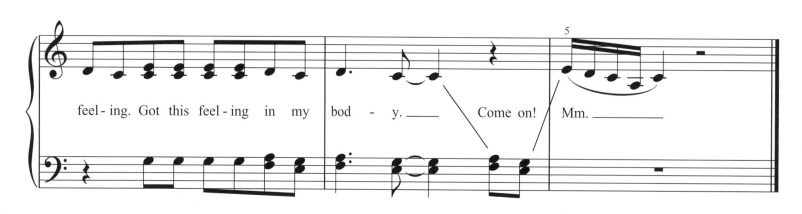

BEST DAY OF MY LIFE

Words and Music by ZACHARY BARNETT,
JAMES ADAM SHELLEY, MATTHEW SANCHEZ,
DAVID RUBLIN, SHEP GOODMAN
and AARON ACCETTA

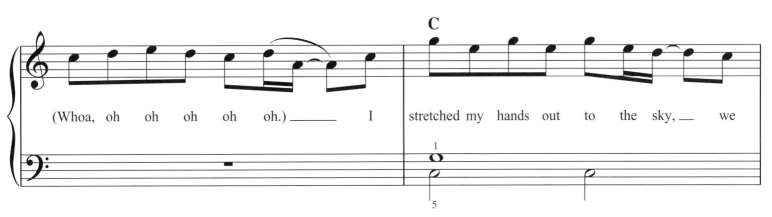

danced with mon - sters through the night. _____ Whoa, oh oh oh oh oh. _____

(Whoa, oh oh oh oh oh.) _____ I'm nev - er gon - na look back, whoa. _ I'm

nev - er gon - na give it up, no. _____ Please don't wake me now. __

Woo, woo, _____ woo. This is gon - na be the best day of my

life. _____ My life. _____ Woo, woo, _____

woo. This is gon - na be the best day of my life. _____ My

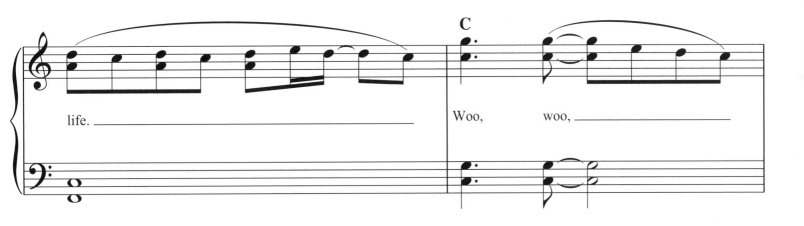

life. _____ Woo, woo, _____

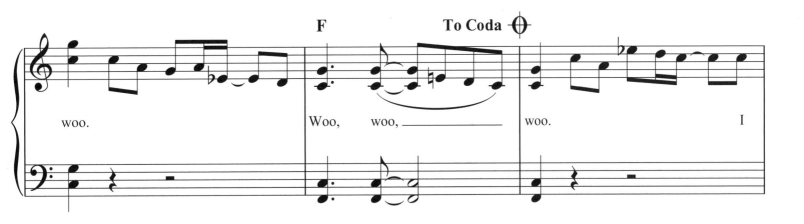

woo. Woo, woo, _____ woo. I

howled at the moon with friends and then the sun came crash-ing in.

Whoa, oh oh oh oh oh. (Whoa, oh oh oh oh oh.) But

all the pos - si - bil - i - ties, no lim - its just e - piph - a - nies.

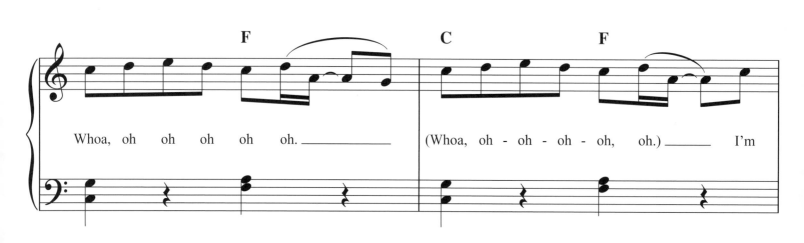

Whoa, oh oh oh oh oh. (Whoa, oh - oh - oh - oh, oh.) I'm

Am

nev - er gon - na look back, whoa. _ I'm

C

nev - er gon - na give it up, no. _____

F

Just don't wake me now.

D.S. al Coda

CODA

woo.

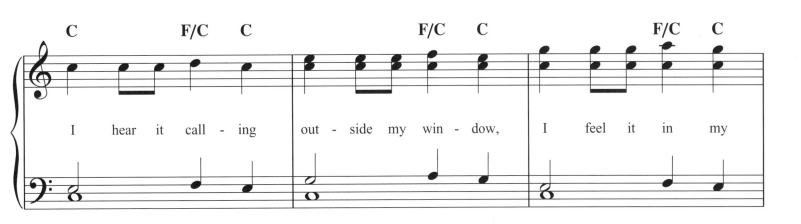

C   **F/C**   **C**   **F/C**   **C**   **F/C**   **C**

I hear it call - ing   out - side my win - dow,   I feel it in my

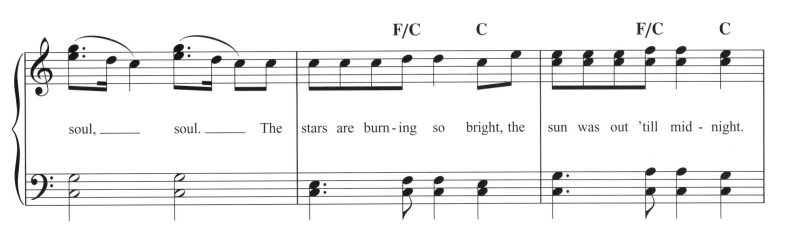

                        F/C   **C**   **F/C**   **C**

soul, _____ soul. _____ The   stars are burn - ing so bright, the   sun was out 'till mid - night.

I say we lose con - trol, _____ con - trol. _____

Woo, woo, _____ woo, _____ woo. _____

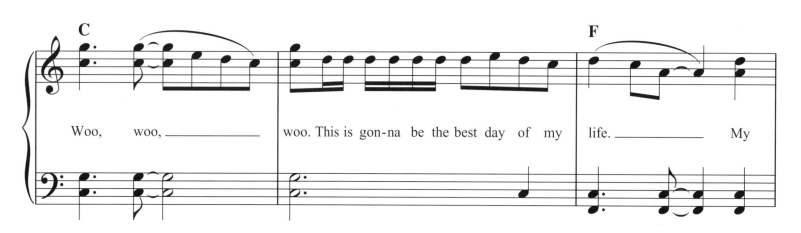

Woo, woo, _____ woo. This is gon-na be the best day of my life. _____ My

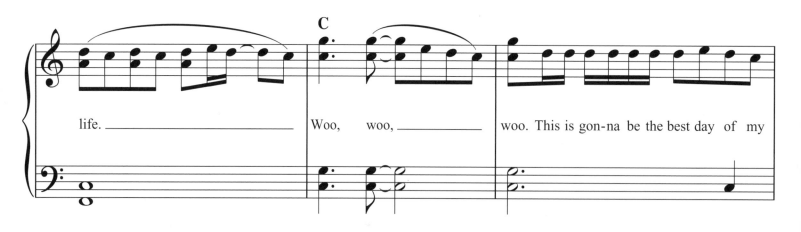

life. _____ Woo, woo, _____ woo. This is gon-na be the best day of my

life. _____ My | life. _____ Woo, woo. _____

Ev-'ry-thing is look-ing up, ev-'ry-bod-y up now. Woo, woo. _____

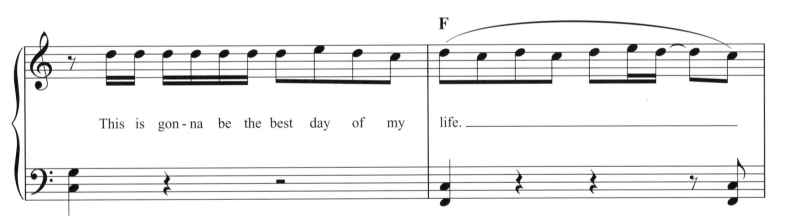

This is gon-na be the best day of my | life. _____

This is gon-na be the best day of my | life. _____

BRAVE

Words and Music by SARA BAREILLES
and JACK ANTONOFF

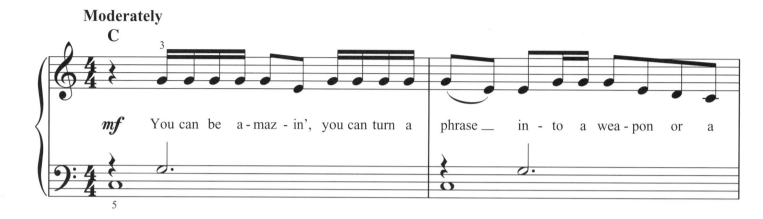

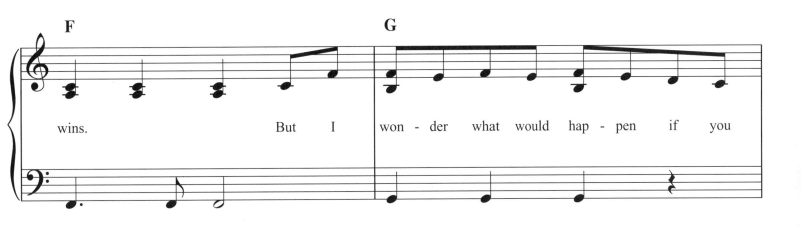

out   hon-est-ly.   I wan-na see you be brave.___   Just wan-na see you.

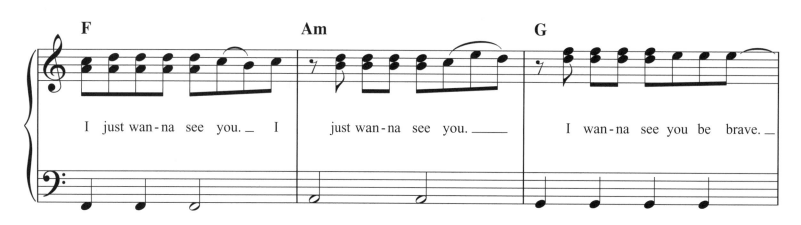

I just wan-na see you. _ I   just wan-na see you._____   I wan-na see you be brave._

___ Just wan-na see you.   I just wan-na see you. _ I   just wan-na see you,_____

I wan-na see you be   brave.

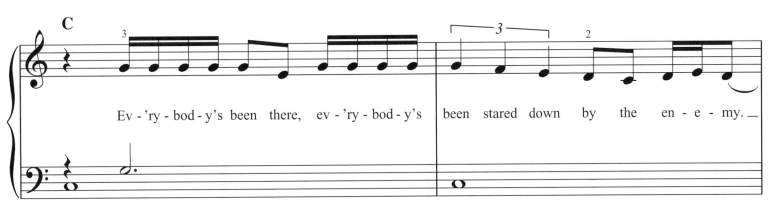

in and show — me — how big your brave — is. Say what you wan-na say

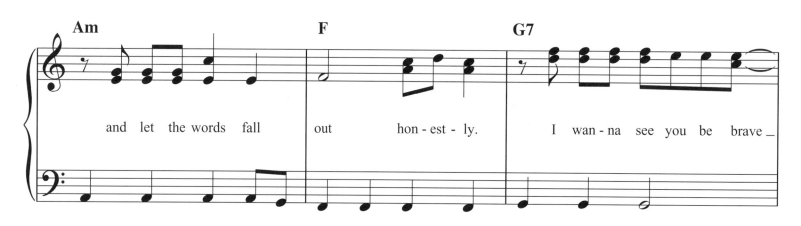

and let the words fall out hon-est-ly. I wan-na see you be brave —

— with what you wan-na say and let the words fall out hon-est-ly.

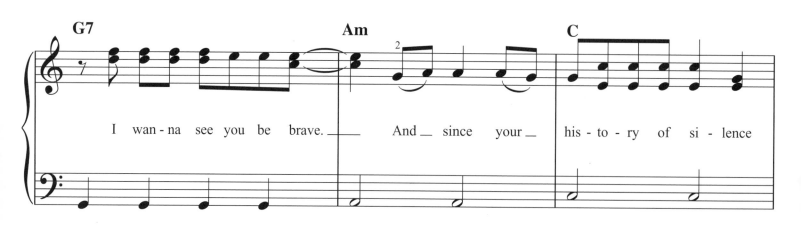

I wan-na see you be brave. — And — since your — his-to-ry of si-lence

FEEL AGAIN

Words and Music by RYAN TEDDER,
NOEL ZANCANELLA, BRENT KUTZLE
and ANDREW BROWN

just can't ring. — } I reached out try'n to love — but I feel noth - ing. —
just can't sing. —

{ Yeah, } my heart — is numb. — But with you _____
{ Oh, }

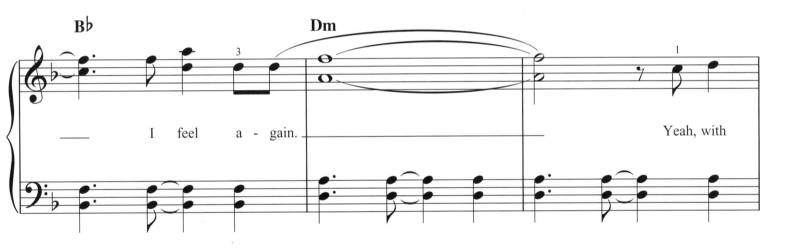

_____ I feel a - gain. _____ Yeah, with

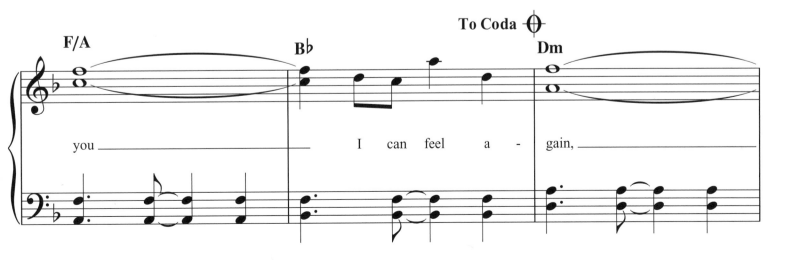

To Coda ⊕

you _____ I can feel a - gain, _____

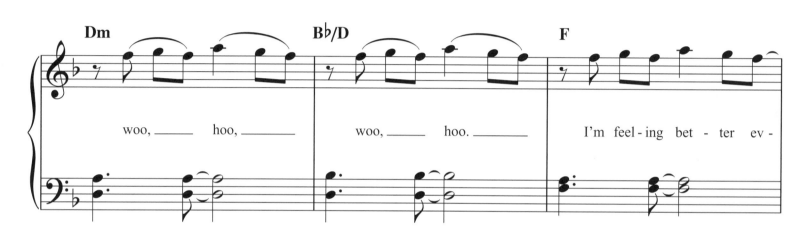

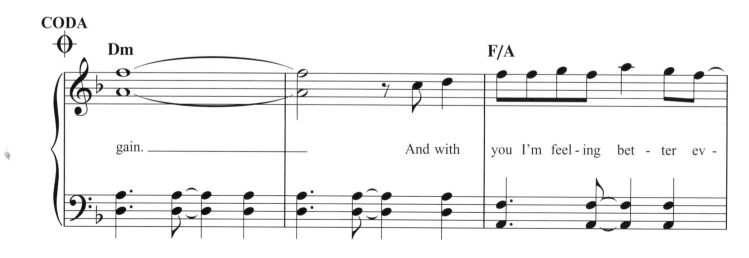

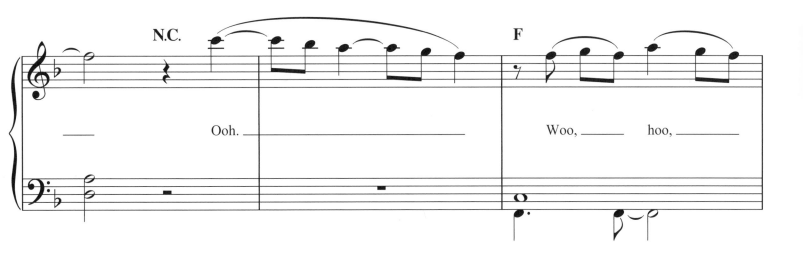

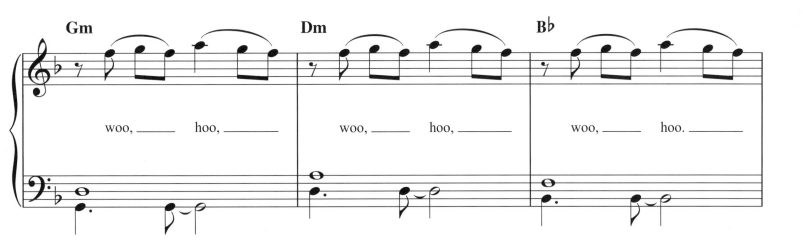

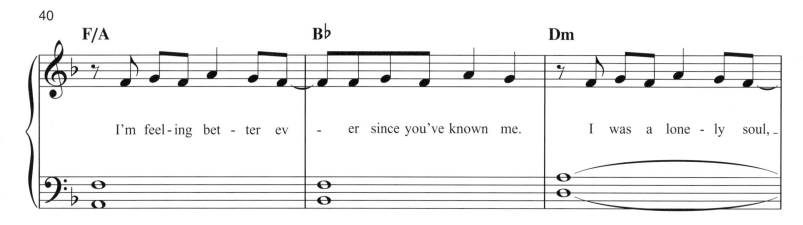

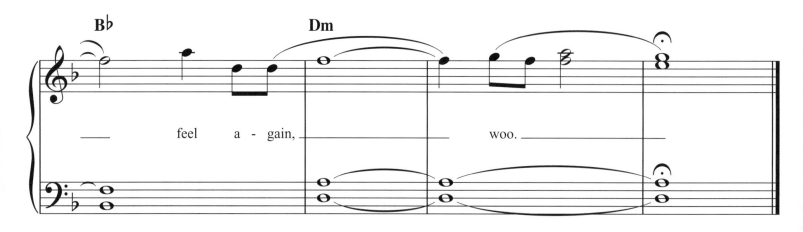

COOL KIDS

Words and Music by GRAHAM SIEROTA,
JAMIE SIEROTA, NOAH SIEROTA,
SYDNEY SIEROTA, JEFFREY DAVID SIEROTA
and JESIAH DZWONEK

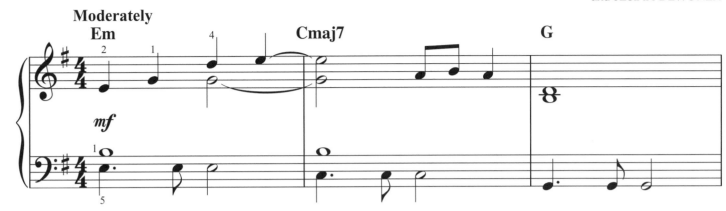

She sees 'em walk-in' in a straight line,
He sees 'em talk-in' with a big smile,

that's not real-ly her __ style. __ And they all
but they have-n't got a clue. __ Yeah, they're

got the same heart - beat,
liv - in' the good ___ life,

but hers is fall - ing be -
can't see what he is go - in'

hind. _____
through. _____

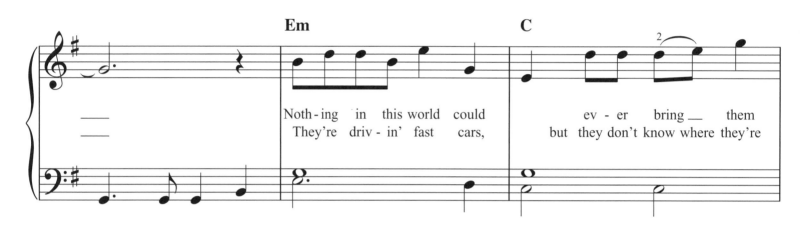

Em   **C**

_____
_____

Noth - ing in this world could
They're driv - in' fast cars,

ev - er bring ___ them
but they don't know where they're

G   **Em**

down. _____
go - ing, _____

Yeah, they're in - vin - ci - ble,
in the fast ___ lane,

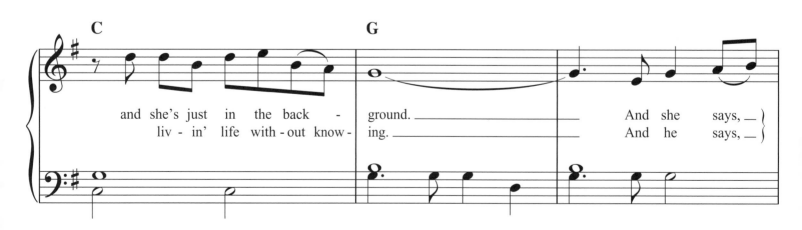

C   **G**

and she's just in the back -
liv - in' life with - out know -

ground. _____
ing. _____

And she says, ___ }
And he says, ___ }

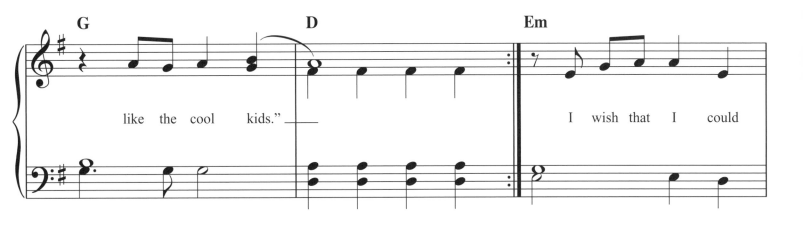

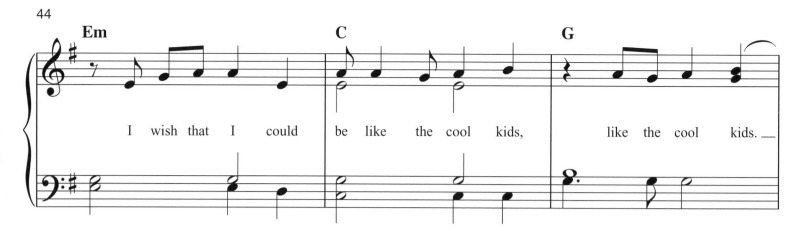

I wish that I could be like the cool kids, like the cool kids.

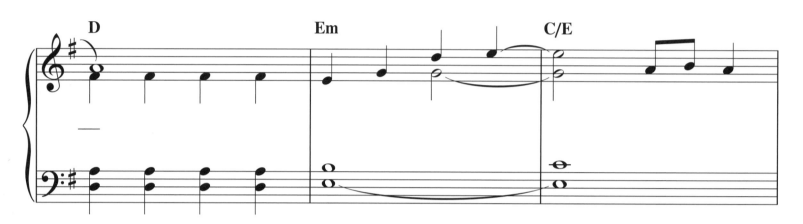

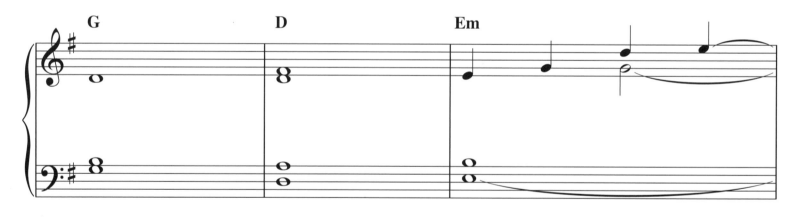

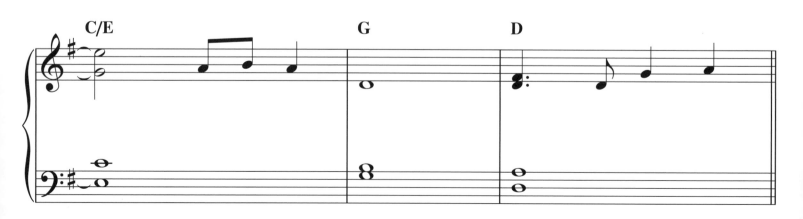

I wish that I could be like the cool kids, 'cause all the cool kids,

they seem to { fit in / get it. } I wish that I could be like the cool kids,

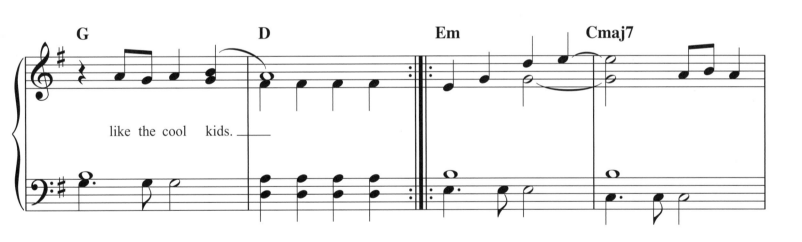

like the cool kids.

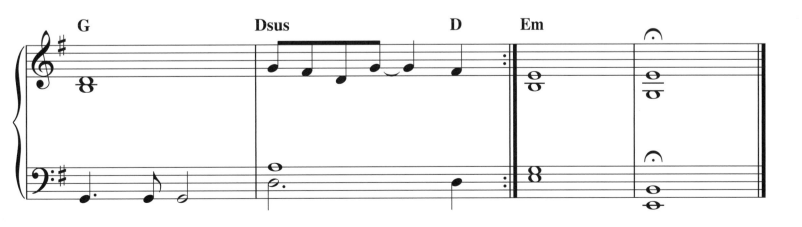

FIREWORK

Words and Music by KATY PERRY,
MIKKEL ERIKSEN, TOR ERIK HERMANSEN,
ESTHER DEAN and SANDY WILHELM

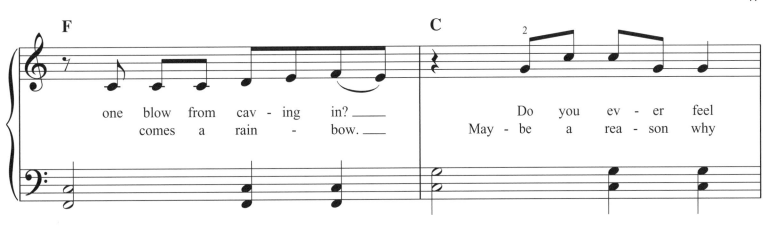

one blow from cav - ing in? _____
comes a rain - bow. _____

Do you ev - er feel
May - be a rea - son why

al - read - y bur - ied deep,
all the doors were closed.

six feet un - der screams, but
So you could o - pen one that

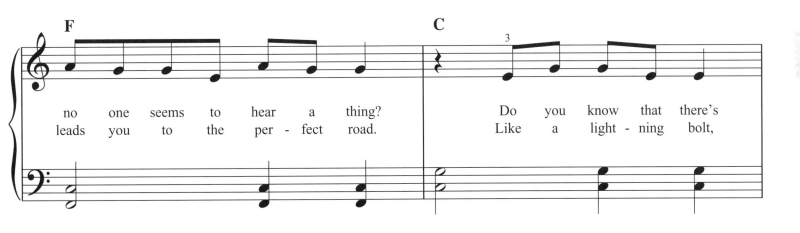

no one seems to hear a thing?
leads you to the per - fect road.

Do you know that there's
Like a light - ning bolt,

still a chance for you?
your heart will glow;

'Cause there's a spark in you.
and when it's time, you'll know.

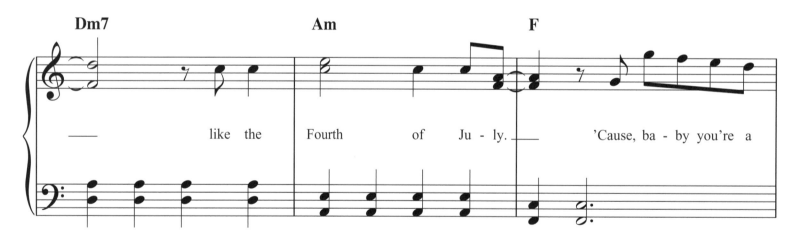

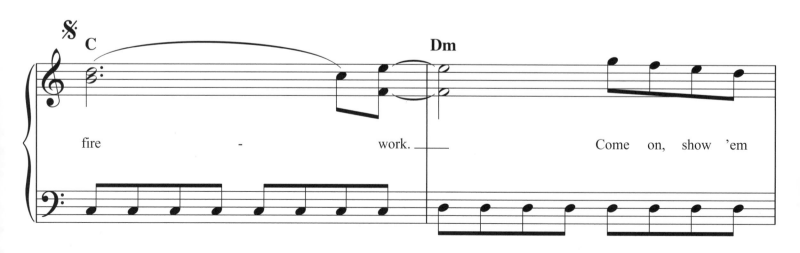

what you're worth. ___ Make 'em go, ___ "Aah, aah, ___ aah,"

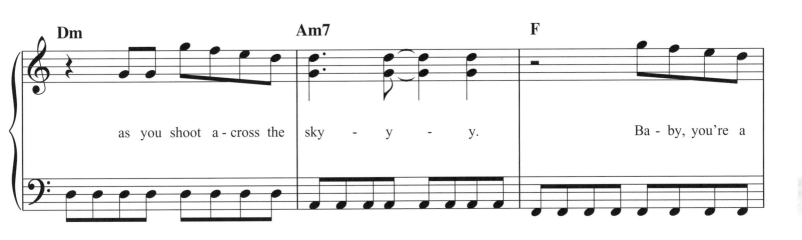

as you shoot a-cross the sky - y - y. Ba-by, you're a

fire - work. ___ Come on, let your col - ors burst. ___

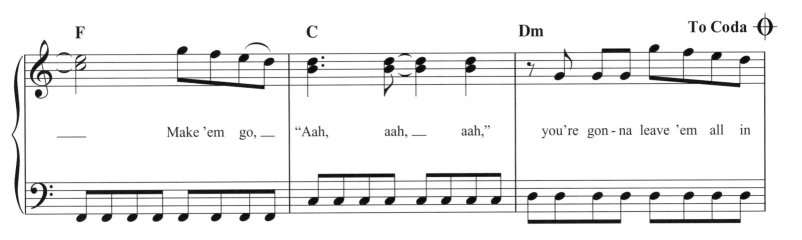

Make 'em go, ___ "Aah, aah, ___ aah," you're gon-na leave 'em all in

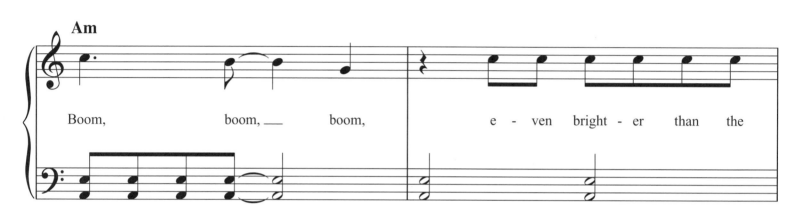

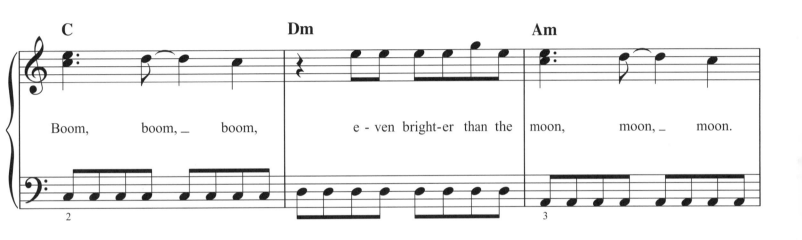

HOME

Words and Music by GREG HOLDEN
and DREW PEARSON

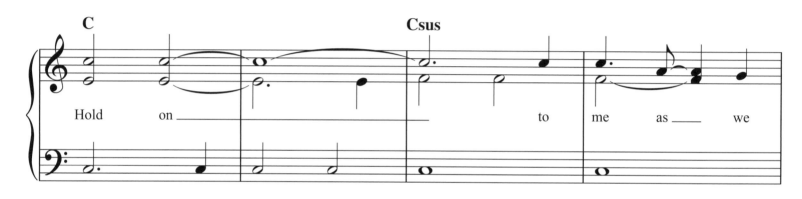

Hold on _____ to me as ____ we

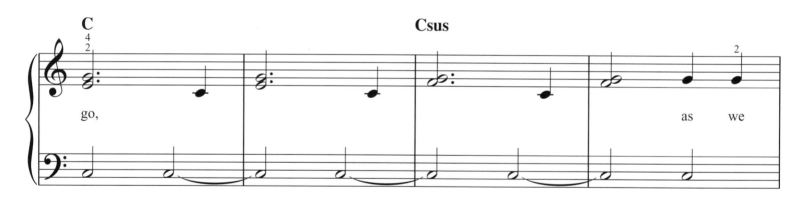

go, as we

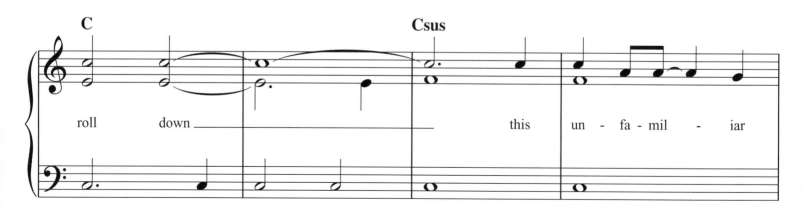

roll down _____ this un - fa - mil - iar

C

road.

Csus

And al - though this

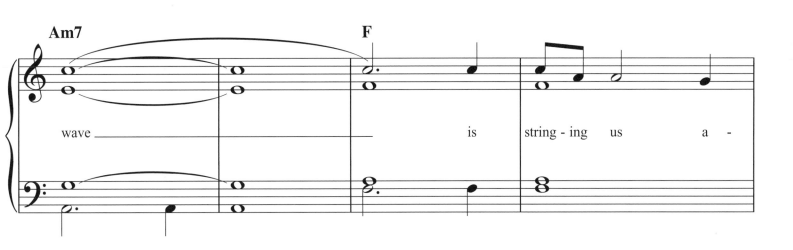

Am7

wave _____

F

is string - ing us a -

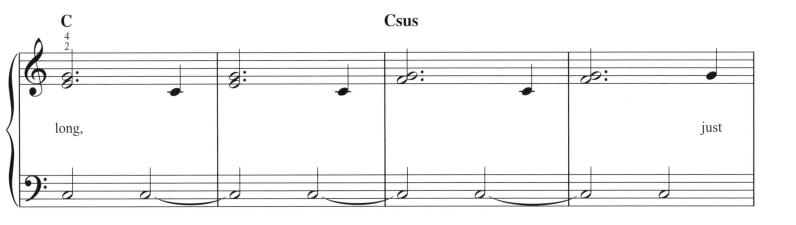

C

long,

Csus

just

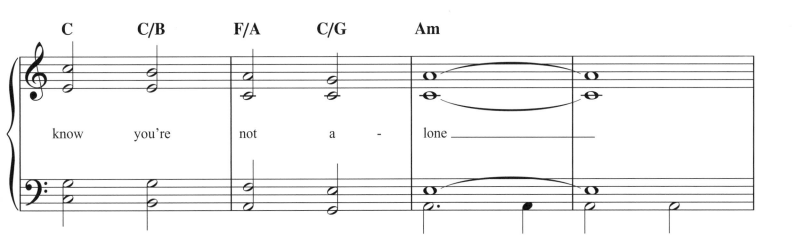

C   **C/B**   **F/A**   **C/G**   **Am**

know   you're   not   a -   lone _____

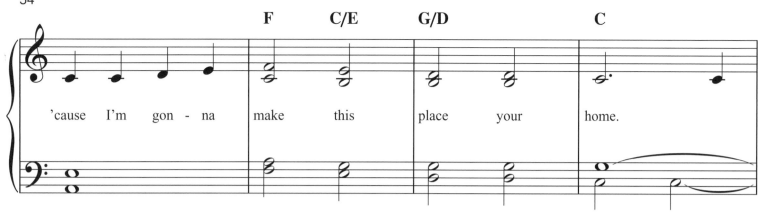

'cause I'm gon - na make this place your home.

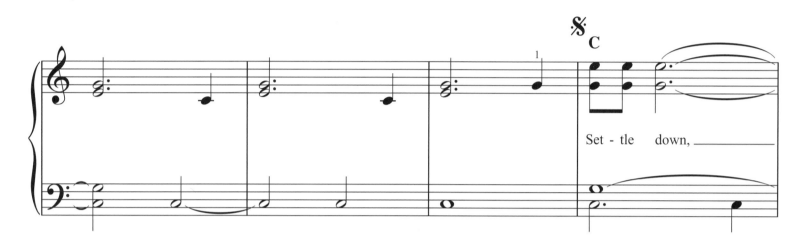

Set - tle down, _____

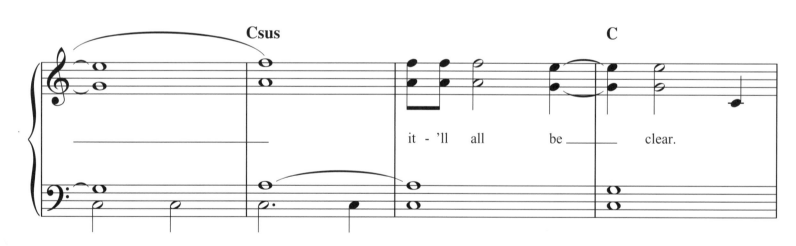

_____ it - 'll all be ____ clear.

Don't pay ___ no

mind to ____ the de - mons; ___ they fill you ___ with fear.

Trou - ble, ___ it

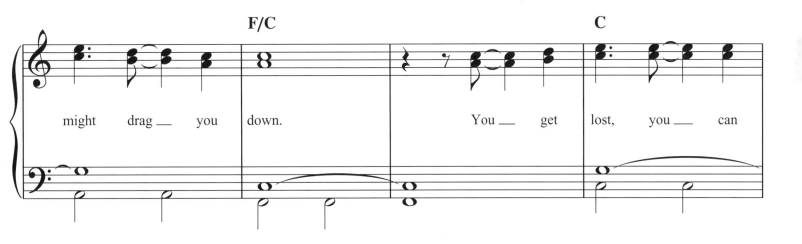

might drag ___ you down. You ___ get lost, you ___ can

al - ways ___ be found. Just know you're

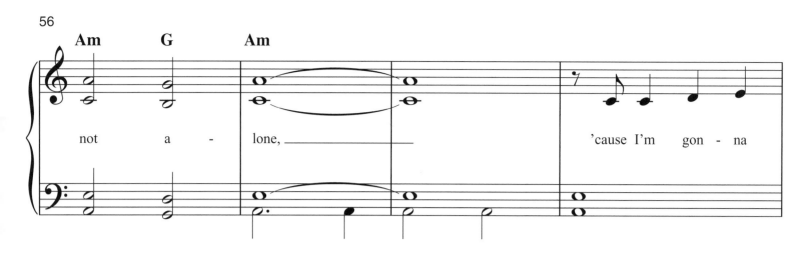

not a - lone,_____ 'cause I'm gon - na

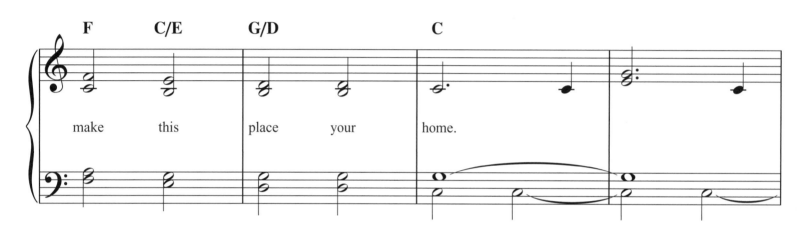

make this place your home.

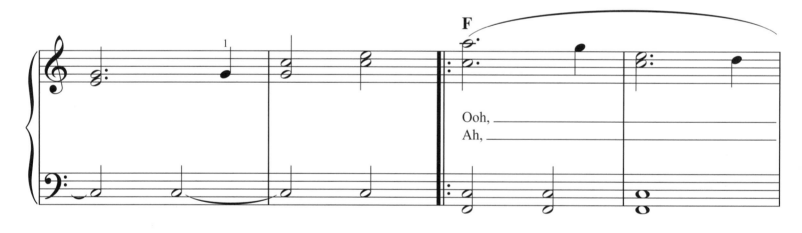

Ooh,_____
Ah,_____

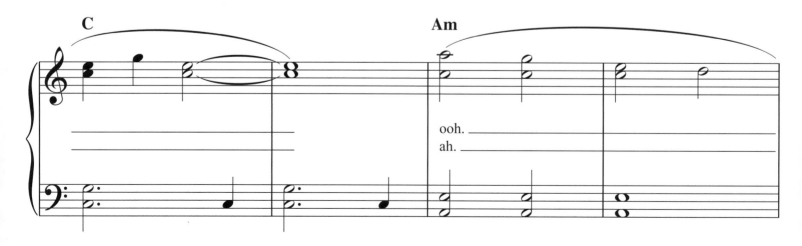

ooh._____
ah._____

To Coda ⊕

Ooh.
Ah.

Ooh.
Ah.

1.

2.

D.S. al Coda

CODA ⊕

Ooh.

HOUSE OF GOLD

Words and Music by
TYLER JOSEPH

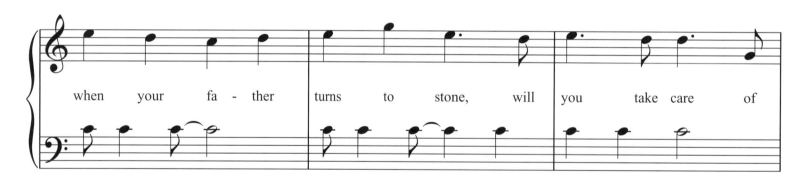

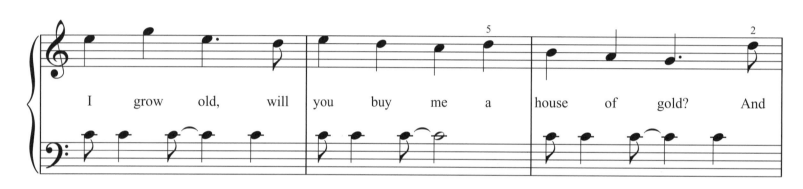

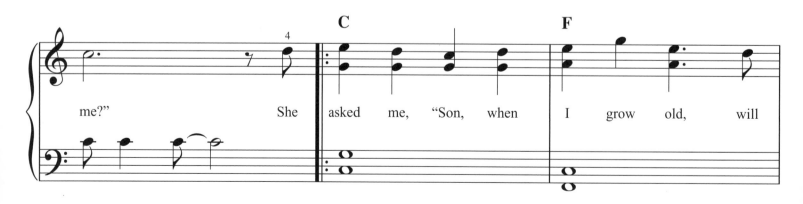

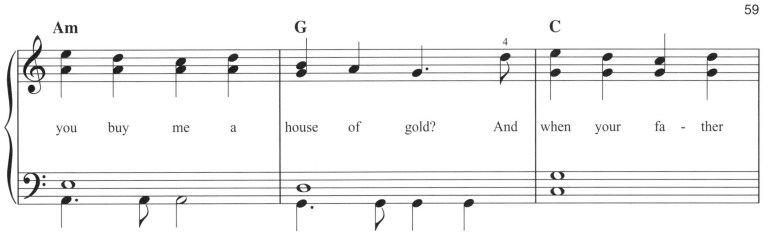

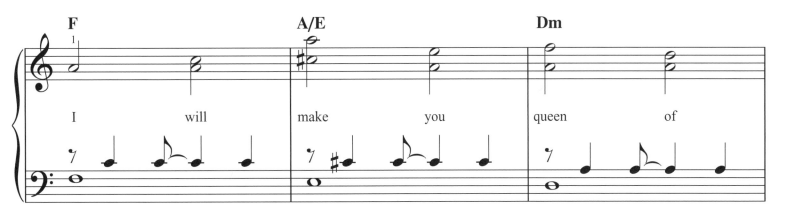

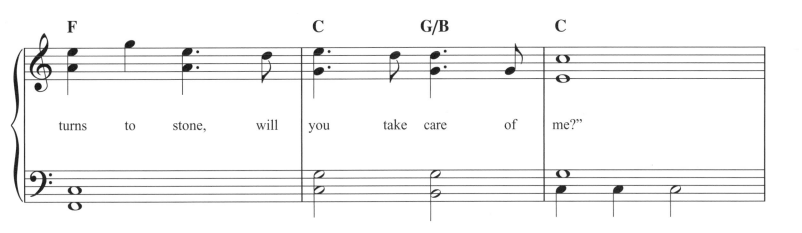

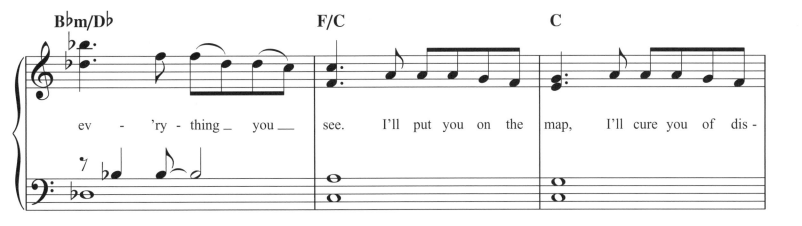

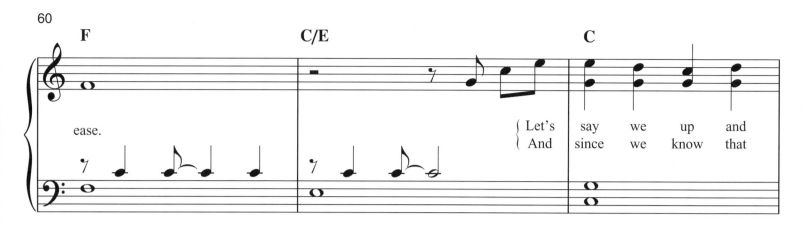

F   **C/E**   **C**

ease.

Let's   say   we   up   and
And   since   we   know   that

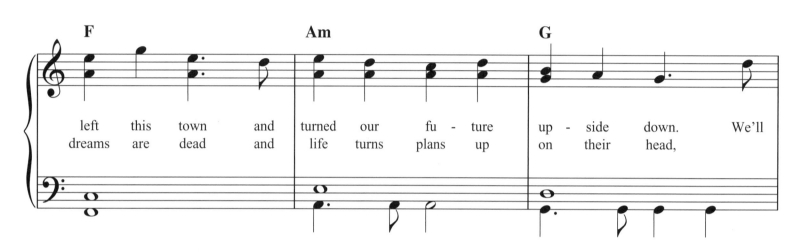

F   **Am**   **G**

left   this   town   and   turned   our   fu - ture   up - side   down.   We'll
dreams   are   dead   and   and   life   turns   plans   up   on   their   head,

C   **F**   **Am**   **G/B**

make   pre - tend   that   you   and   me   lived   ev - er   af - ter
I   will   plan   to   be   a   bum   so   I   just   might   be -

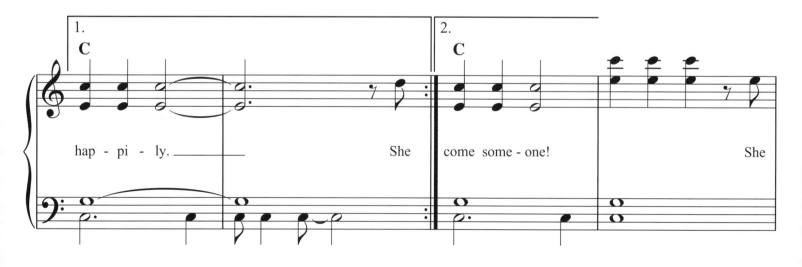

1.
C

hap - pi - ly. _____   She

2.
C

come some - one!   She

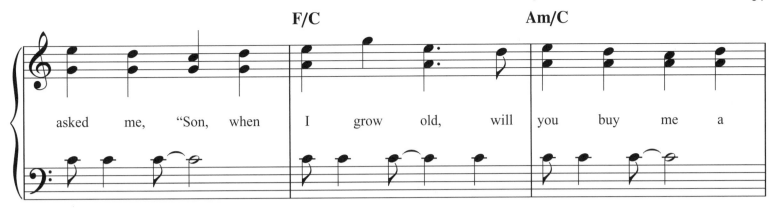

asked me, "Son, when I grow old, will you buy me a

house of gold? And when your fa - ther turns to stone, will you take care of

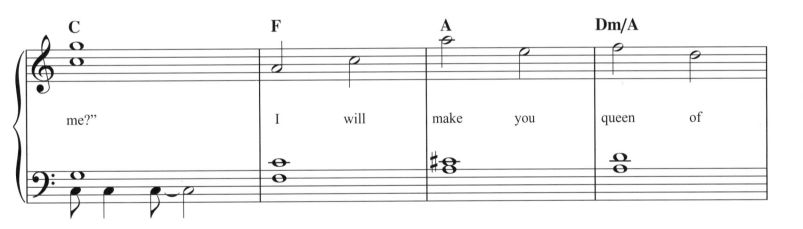

me?" I will make you queen of

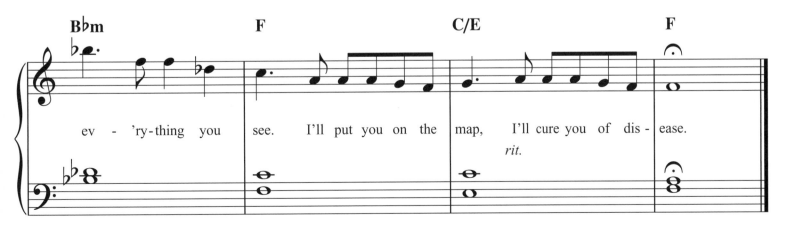

ev - 'ry-thing you see. I'll put you on the map, I'll cure you of dis - ease.

HOW FAR I'LL GO

(Alessia Cara Version)
from MOANA

Music and Lyrics by
LIN-MANUEL MIRANDA

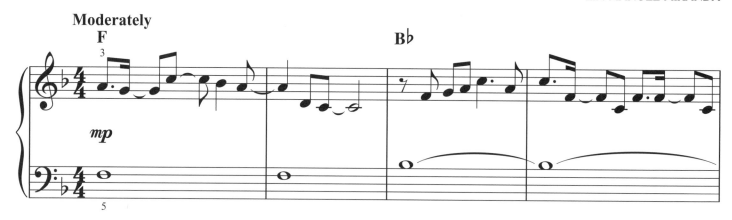

I've been __ star - ing at the edge of the wa - ter __ long __ as I can re-

mem - ber, __ nev - er real - ly know-ing why. I wish __ I could be the per - fect

daugh - ter, __ but I come back to the wa - ter __ no mat-ter how hard I try. Ev - 'ry

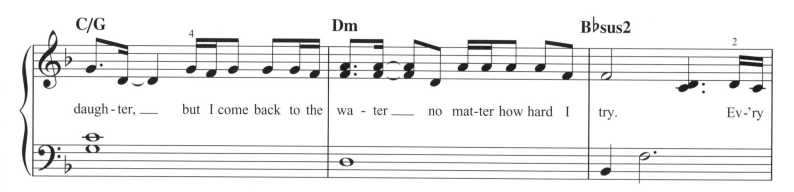

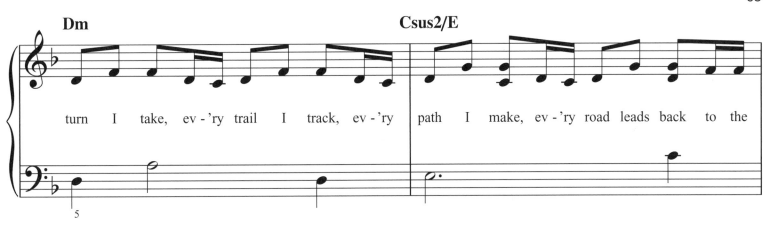

turn I take, ev-'ry trail I track, ev-'ry path I make, ev-'ry road leads back to the

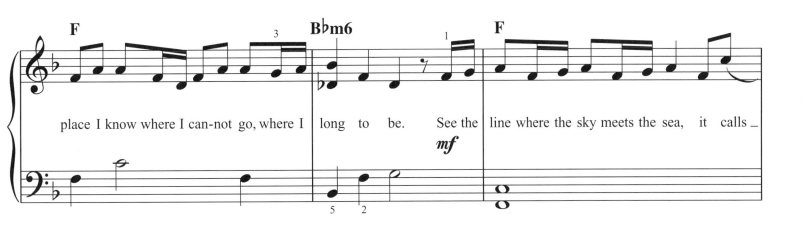

place I know where I can-not go, where I long to be. See the line where the sky meets the sea, it calls

mf

me, and no one knows how far it goes. If the

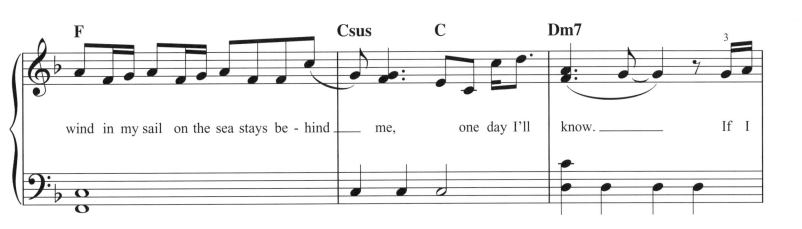

wind in my sail on the sea stays be-hind me, one day I'll know. If I

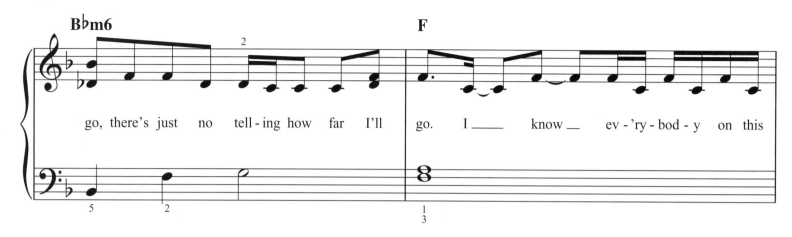

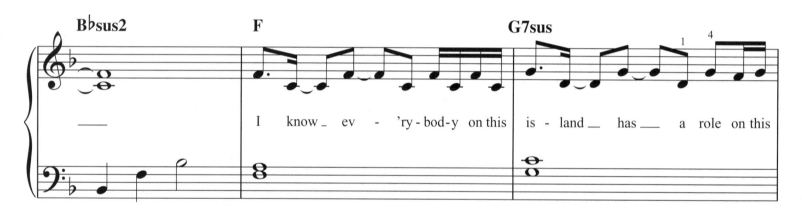

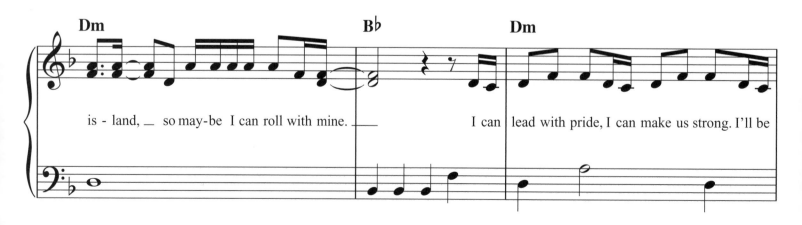

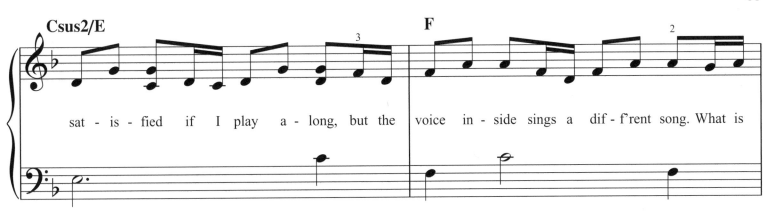

sat - is - fied if I play a - long, but the voice in - side sings a dif - f'rent song. What is

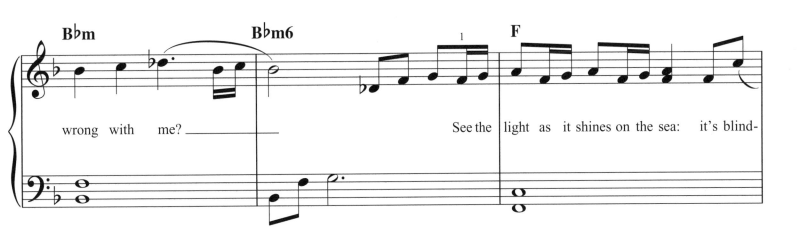

wrong with me? _____ See the light as it shines on the sea: it's blind-

- ing, but no one knows _____ how deep it goes. _____ And it

seems like it's call-ing out to me, so come find _____ me and let me know. _____ What's be-

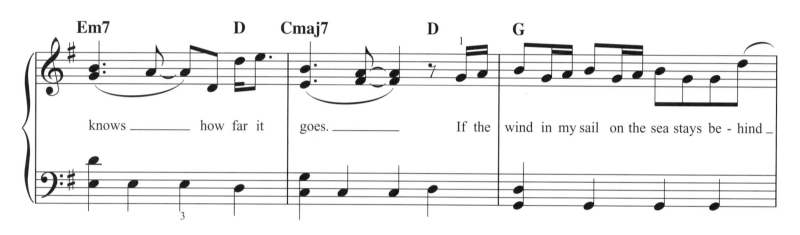

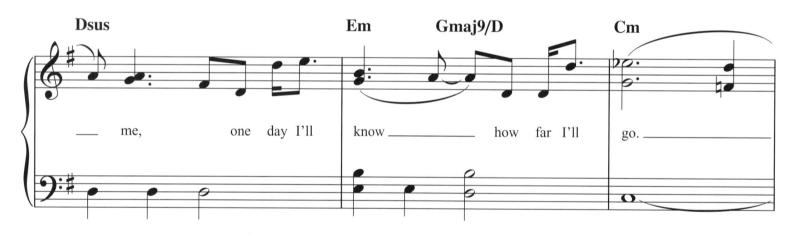

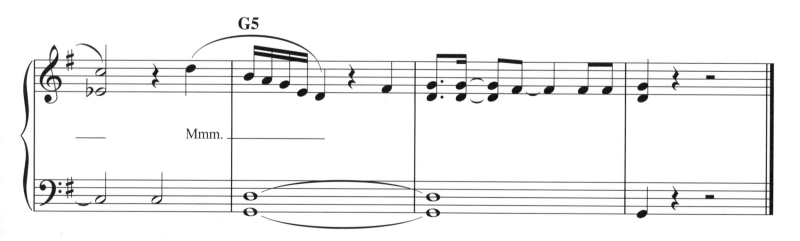

LET IT GO
from FROZEN

Music and Lyrics by KRISTEN ANDERSON-LOPEZ
and ROBERT LOPEZ

Half-time feel, mysterious

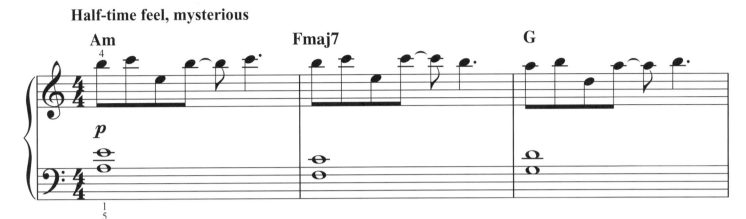

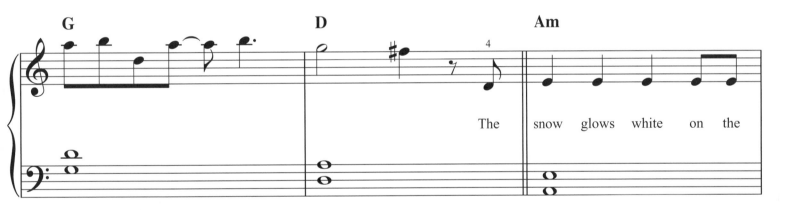

The snow glows white on the

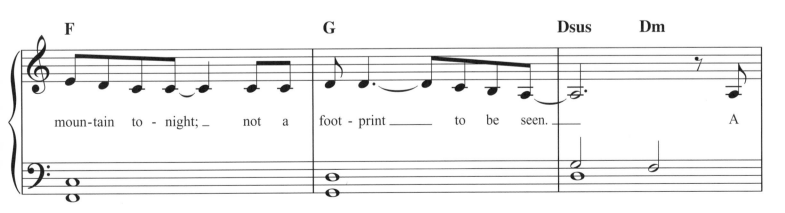

moun-tain to-night;___ not a foot-print_____ to be seen.___ A

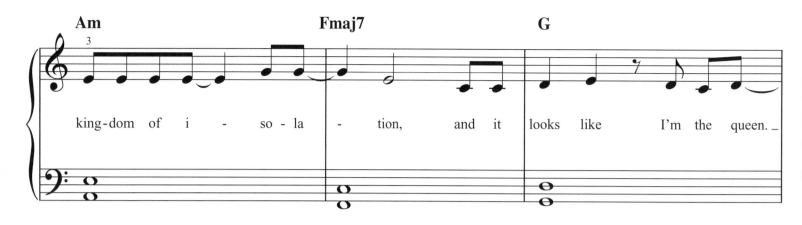

Am ... **Fmaj7** ... **G**

king-dom of i - so - la - tion, and it looks like I'm the queen.

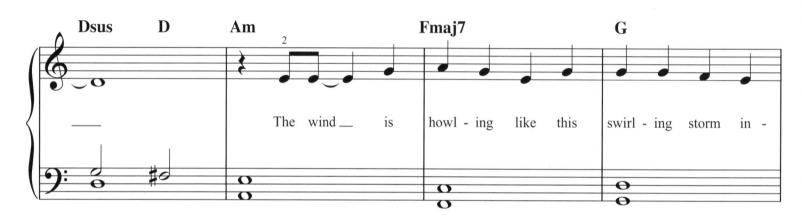

Dsus **D** **Am** ... **Fmaj7** ... **G**

___ The wind __ is howl - ing like this swirl - ing storm in -

Dm ... **Am** ... **G**

side. _____ Could-n't keep it in, ___ heav - en knows I ___

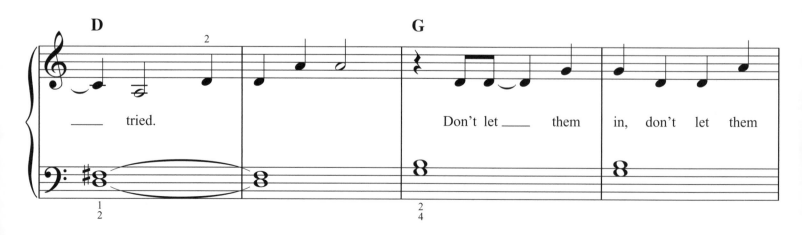

D ... **G**

___ tried. Don't let ___ them in, don't let them

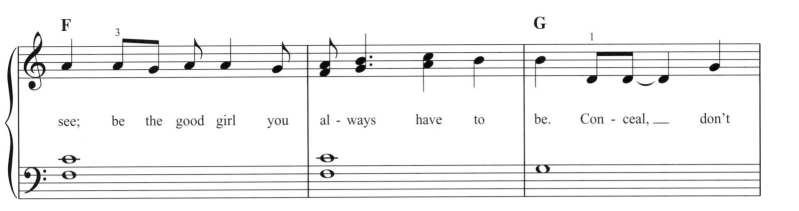

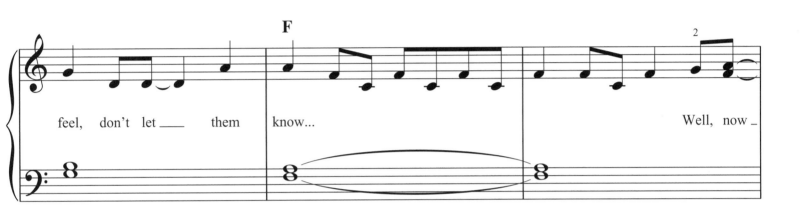

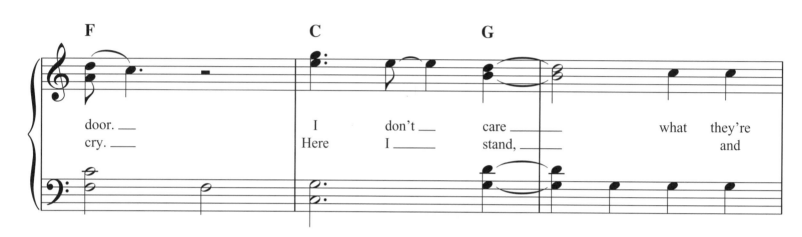

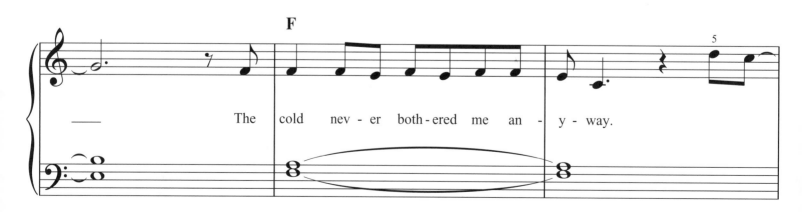

C   G/B   Am

It's fun - ny how some

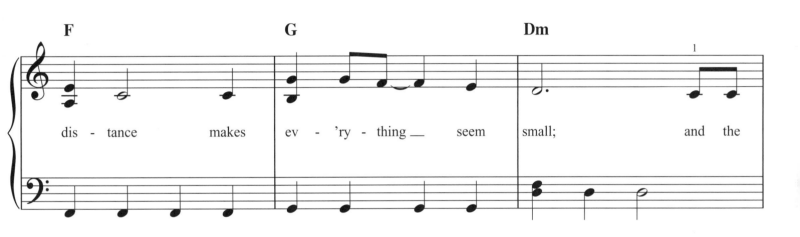

F   G   Dm

dis - tance   makes   ev - 'ry - thing __ seem   small;   and the

Am   F   Dsus

fears that once __ con - trolled me   can't   get   to   me __ at

D   G

all.   It's time __ to   see what I can

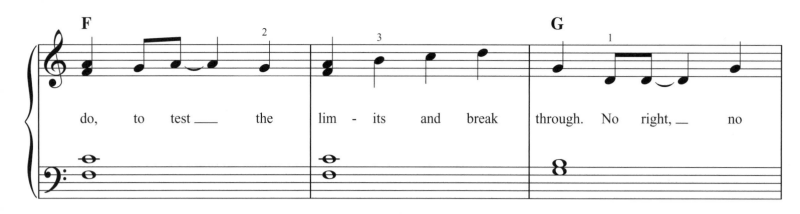

do, to test ___ the lim - its and break through. No right, ___ no

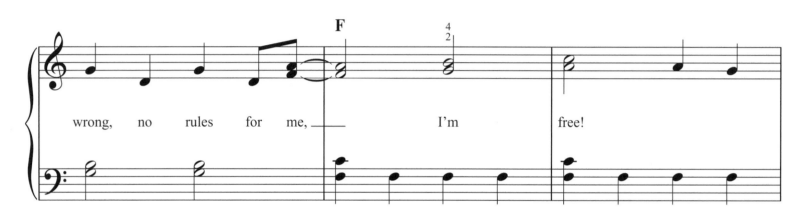

wrong, no rules for me, ___ I'm free!

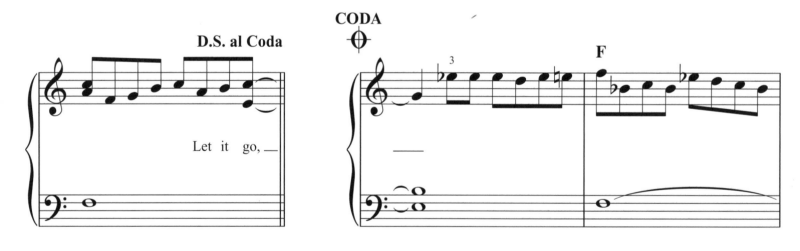

D.S. al Coda

Let it go, ___

CODA

___

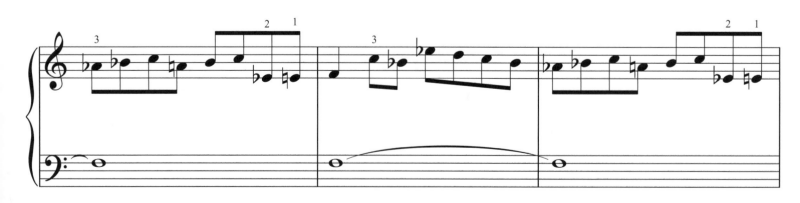

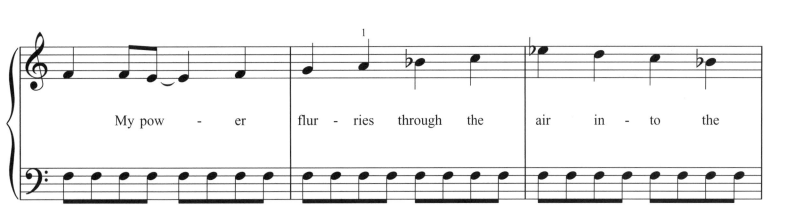

My pow - er flur - ries through the air in - to the

ground. My soul — is spi - ral - ing in

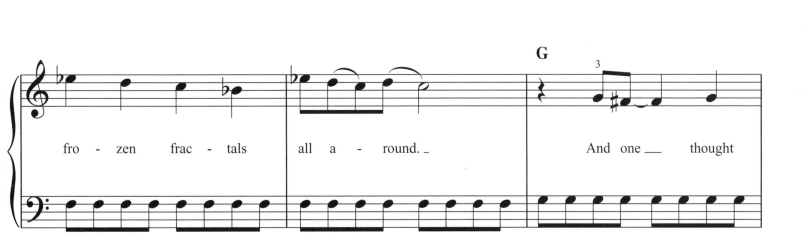

fro - zen frac - tals all a - round. — And one — thought

cry - stal - liz - es like an i - cy blast:

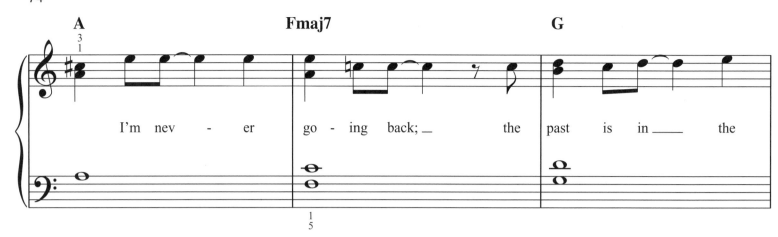

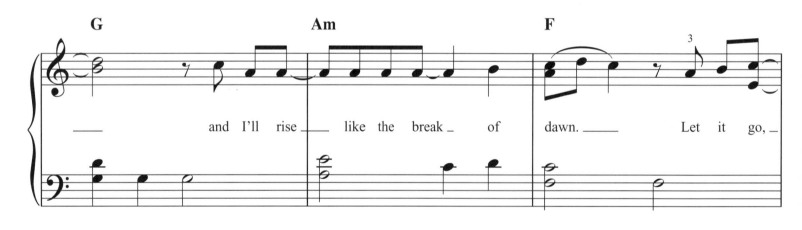

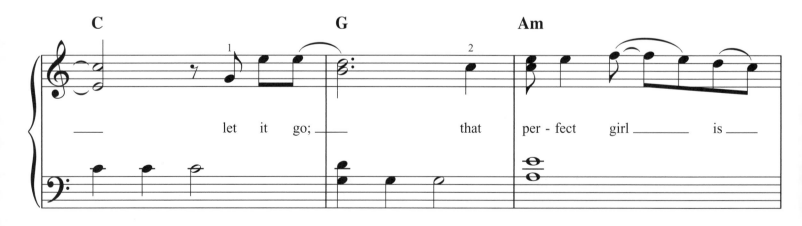

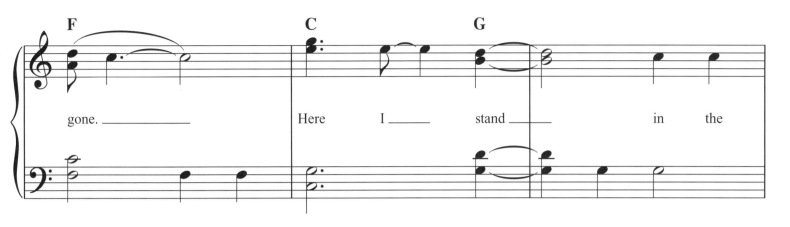

F **C** **G**

gone. _____ Here I ____ stand ____ in the

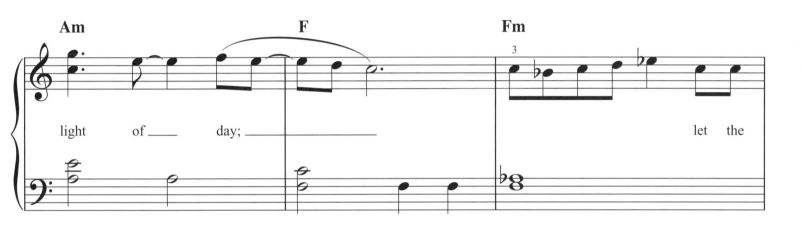

Am **F** **Fm**

light of ___ day; _____ let the

Em **E♭**

storm rage ___ on. _____ The

F

cold nev - er both - ered me an - y - way. _____

ONE CALL AWAY

Words and Music by CHARLIE PUTH,
BREYAN ISAAC, MATT PRIME,
JUSTIN FRANKS, BLAKE ANTHONY CARTER
and MAUREEN McDONALD

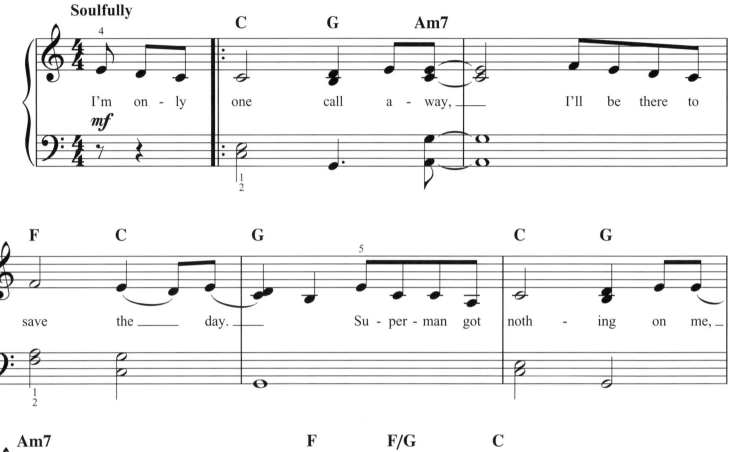

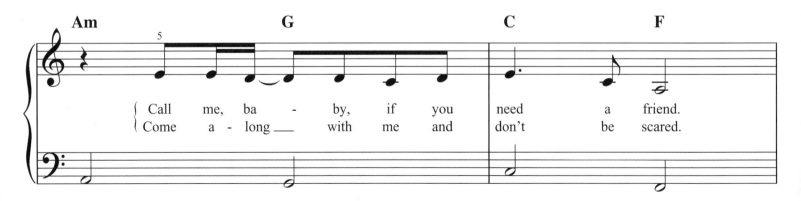

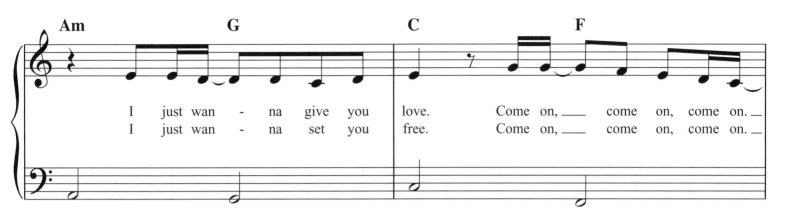

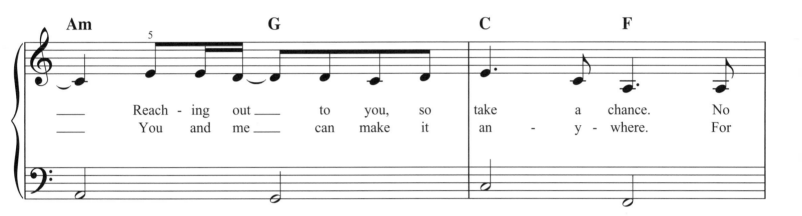

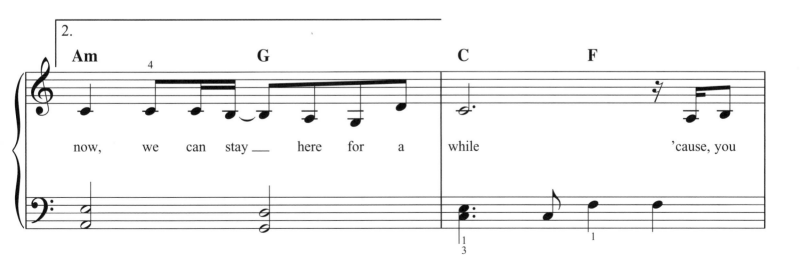

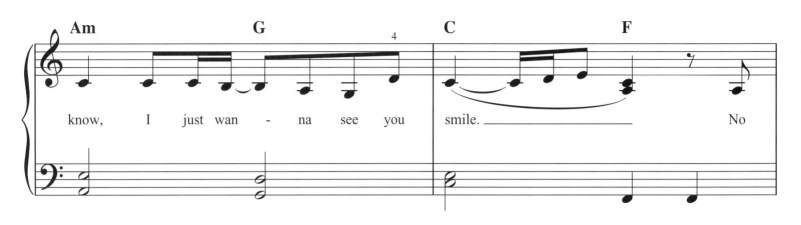

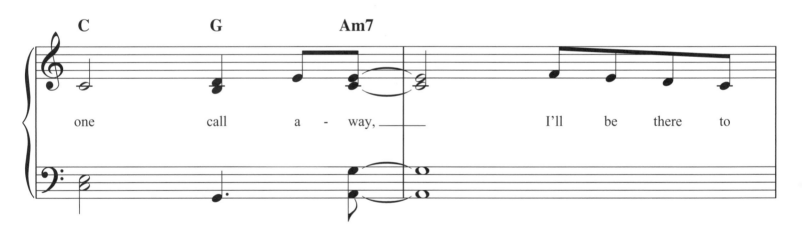

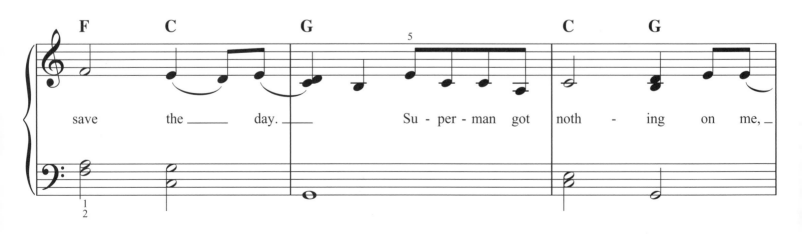

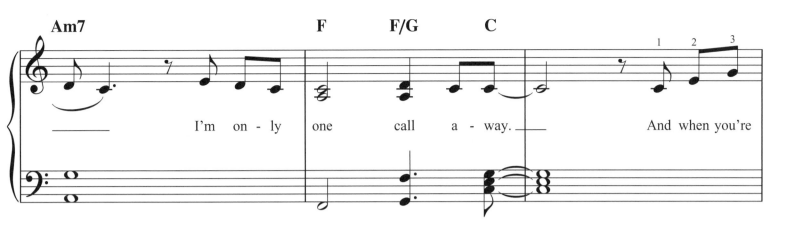

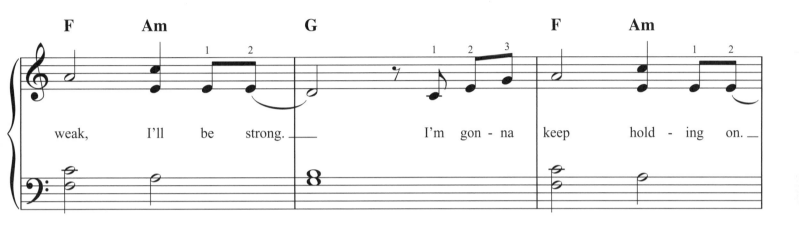

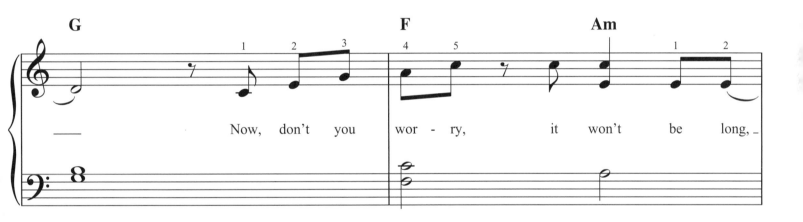

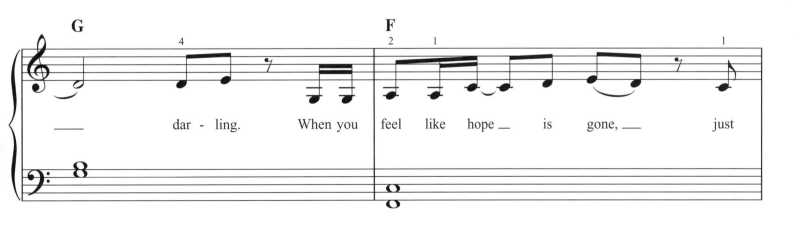

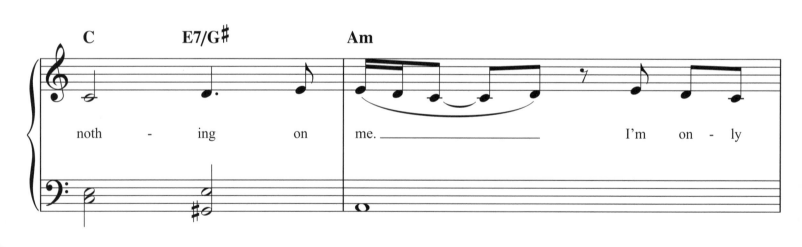

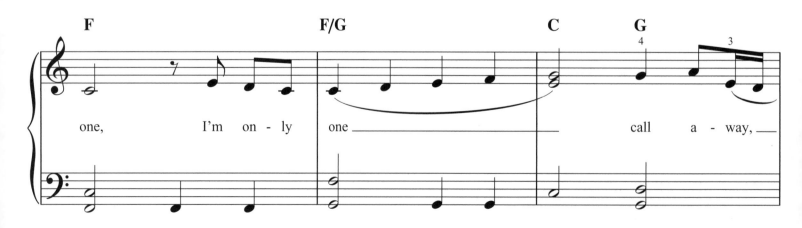

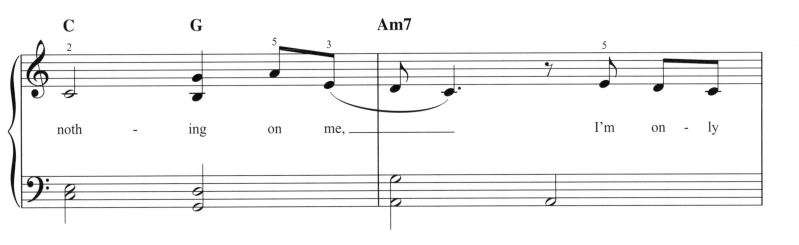

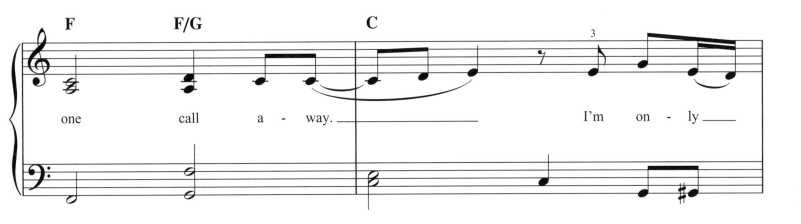

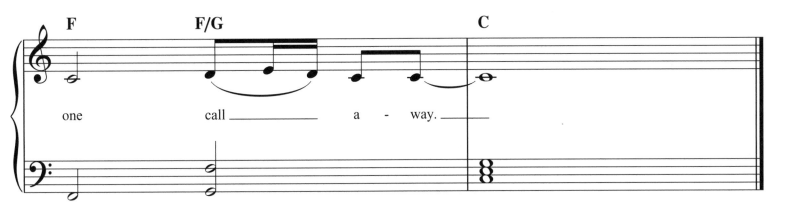

POMPEII

Words and Music by
DAN SMITH

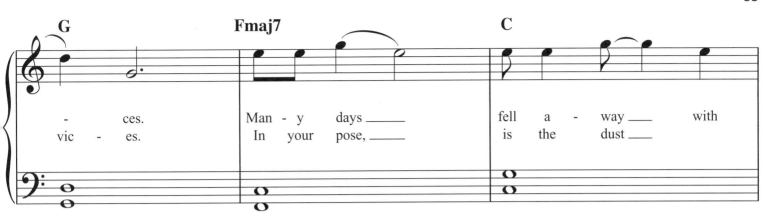

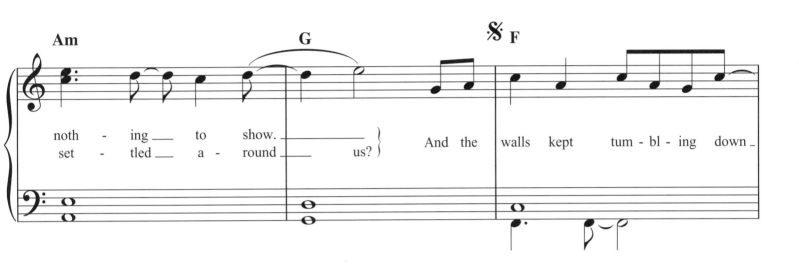

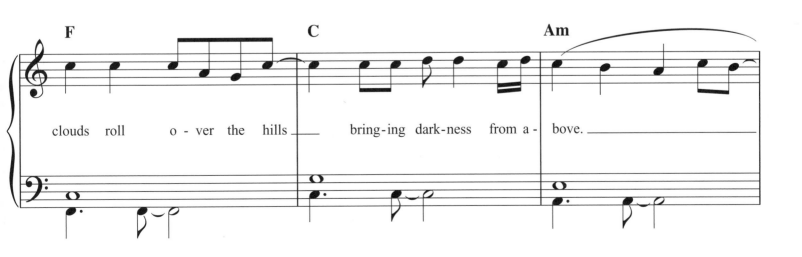

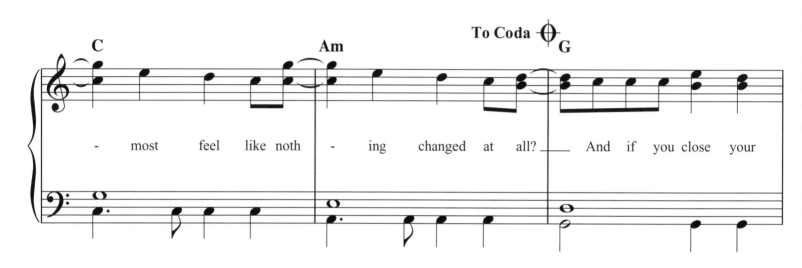

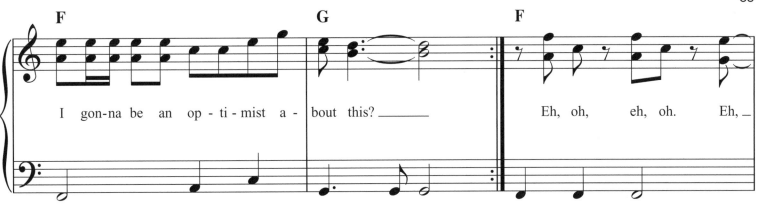

I gon-na be an op-ti-mist a-bout this? _____ Eh, oh, eh, oh. Eh, _____

_____ eh, oh, eh, oh. Eh, _____ eh, oh, eh, oh. Eh, _____ eh, oh, eh, oh. Oh, _____

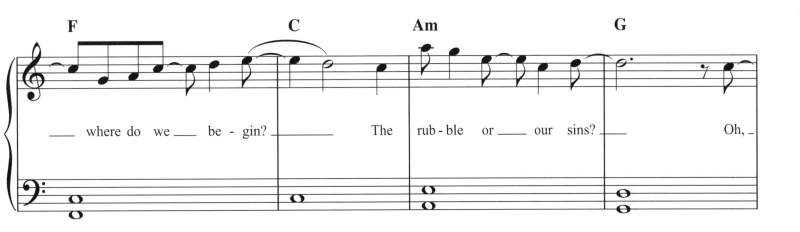

_____ where do we _____ be-gin? _____ The rub-ble or _____ our sins? _____ Oh, _____

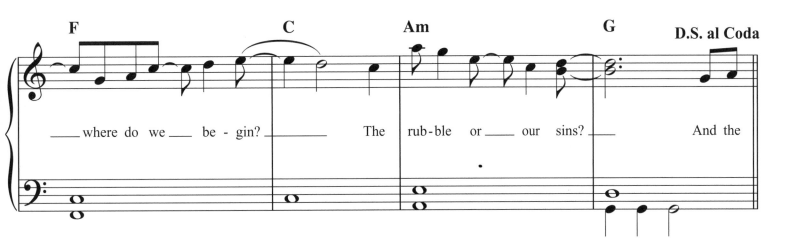

_____ where do we _____ be-gin? _____ The rub-ble or _____ our sins? _____ And the

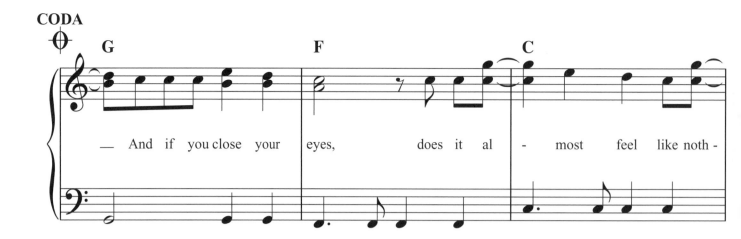

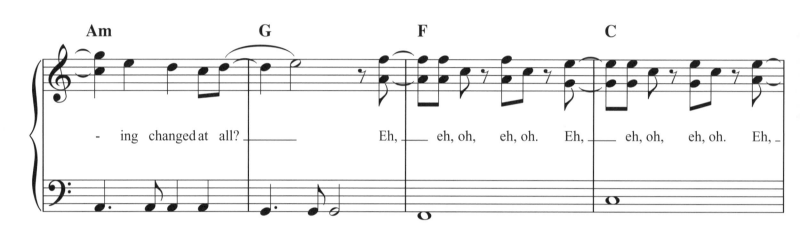

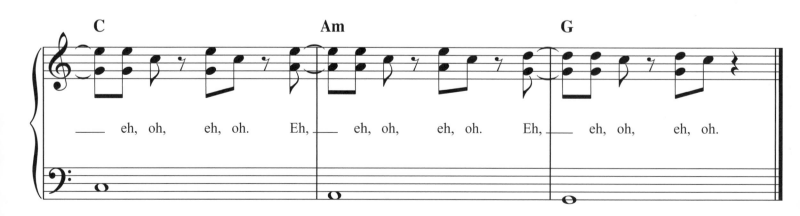

SOMETHING JUST LIKE THIS

Words and Music by ANDREW TAGGART,
CHRIS MARTIN, GUY BERRYMAN,
JOHNNY BUCKLAND and WILL CHAMPION

go? — How much you wan-na risk? I'm not look-ing for some- bod - y with some su-per-hu-man

gifts, some su-per-he - ro, — some fair - y - tale — bliss. Just some-thing I can

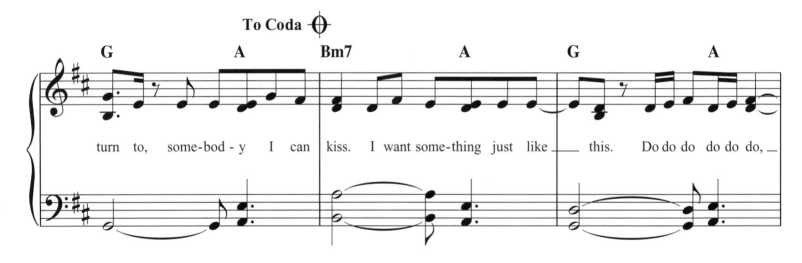

To Coda

turn to, some-bod - y I can kiss. I want some-thing just like — this. Do do do do do do, —

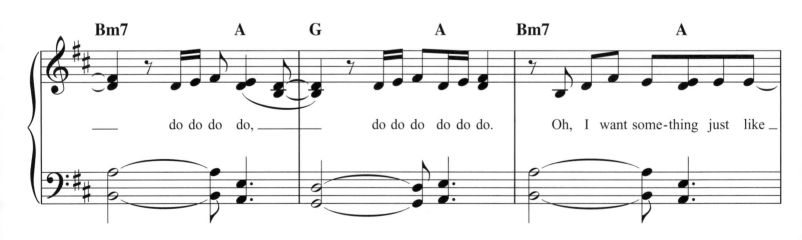

— do do do do, — do do do do do do. Oh, I want some-thing just like —

this. Do do do do do do, _____ do do do do, _____ do do do do do do.

Oh, I want some-thing just like _____ this.

Oh, I want some-thing just like _____ this.

D.S. al Coda

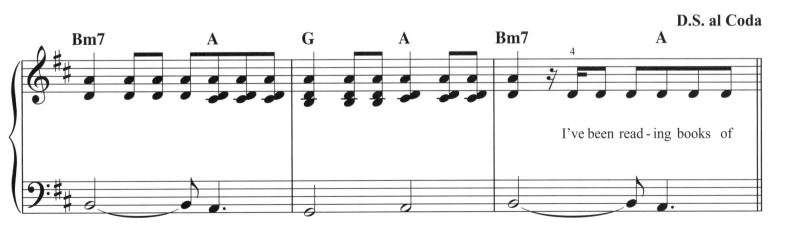

I've been read-ing books of

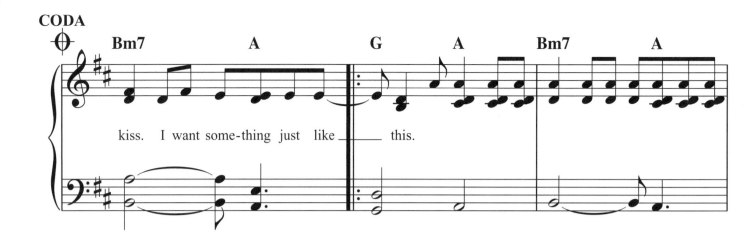

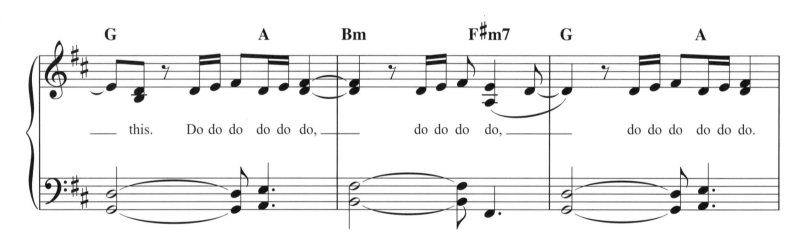

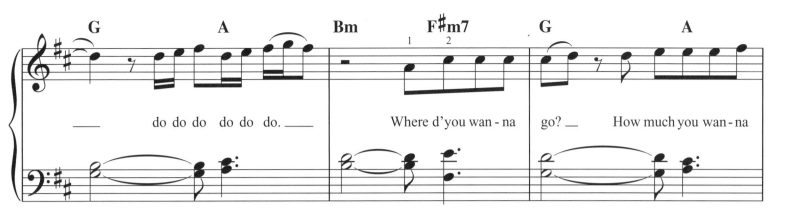

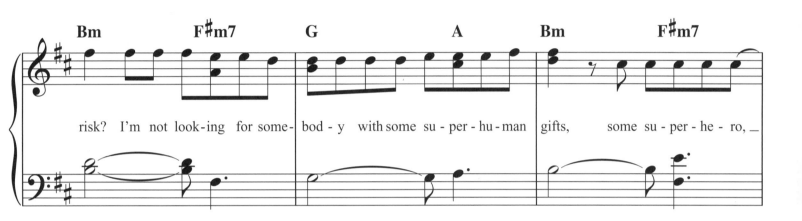

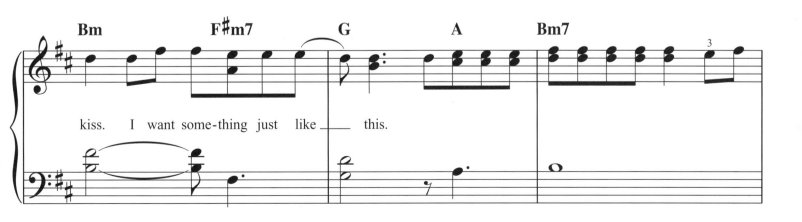

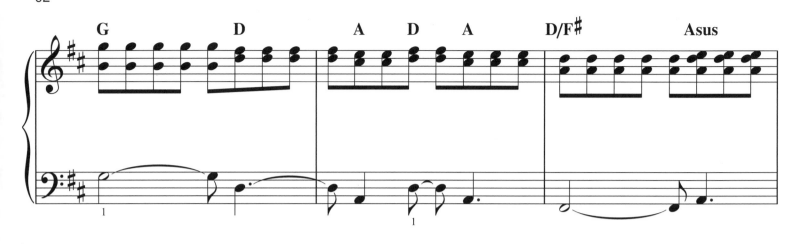

Oh, I want some-thing just like ___

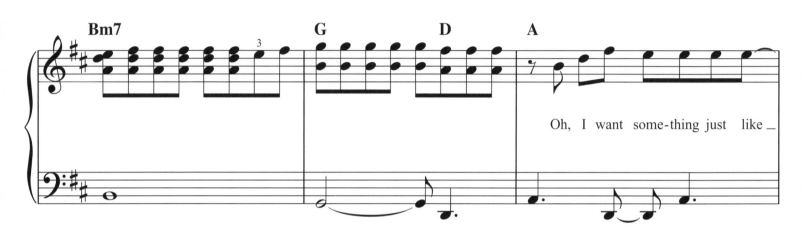

___ this.

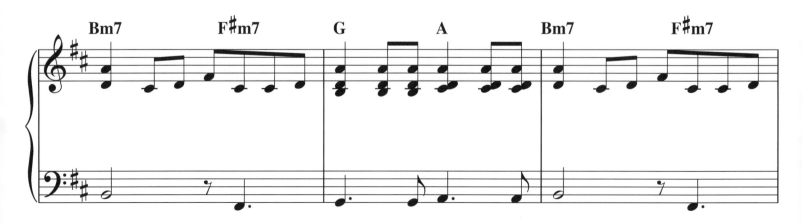

Oh, I want some-thing just like _____ this.

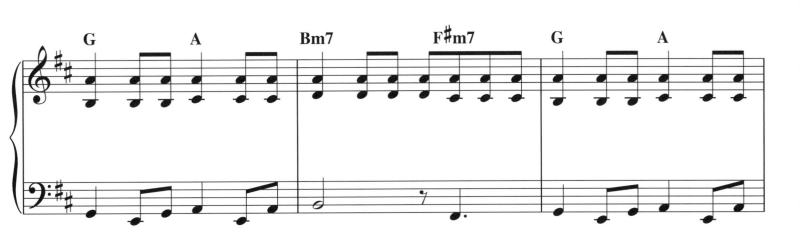

Oh, I want some-thing just like _____ this.

ROAR

Words and Music by KATY PERRY,
MAX MARTIN, DR. LUKE,
BONNIE McKEE and HENRY WALTER

I used to bite my tongue and hold __ my breath, scared to rock the boat and make __ a mess.

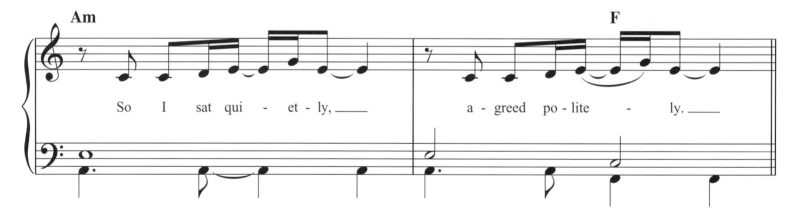

So I sat qui-et-ly, _____ a-greed po-lite - ly. _____

I guess that I for-got I had __ a choice. I let you push me past the break - ing point.
Now I'm float-in' like a but-ter-fly. Sting-in' like a bee, I earned __ my stripes.

I stood for noth - ing, ____ so I fell for ev - 'ry - thing. __ } You
I went from ze - ro ____ to my own he - ro. ____

held me down, but I got up. Al - read - y brush-ing off the dust. You

hear my voice, you hear that sound __ like thun-der gon - na shake the ground. You

held me down, but I got up. Get read - y 'cause I've had e - nough. I

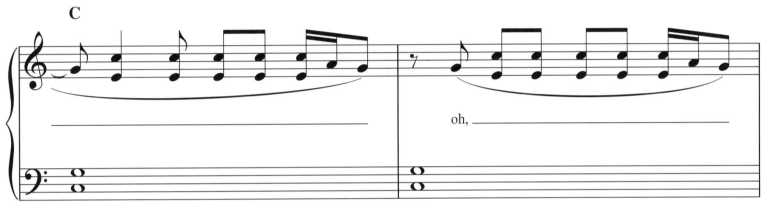

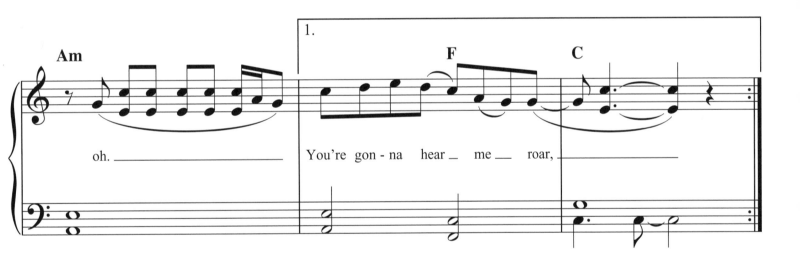

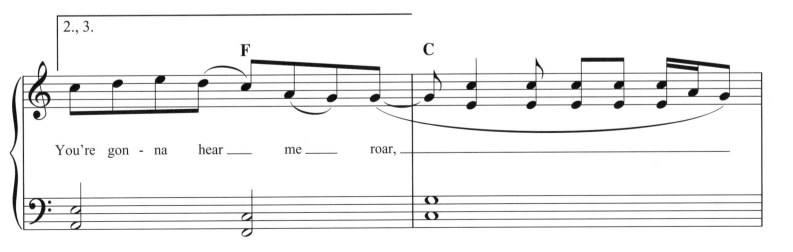

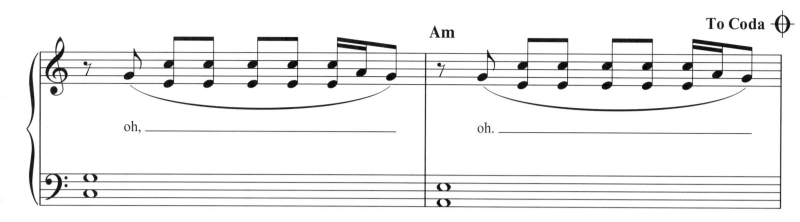

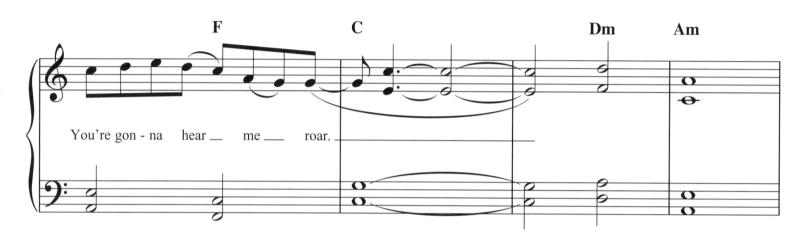

STEREO HEARTS

Words and Music by TRAVIS McCOY,
ADAM LEVINE, BRANDON LOWRY,
DANIEL OMELIO, BENJAMIN LEVIN
and AMMAR MALIK

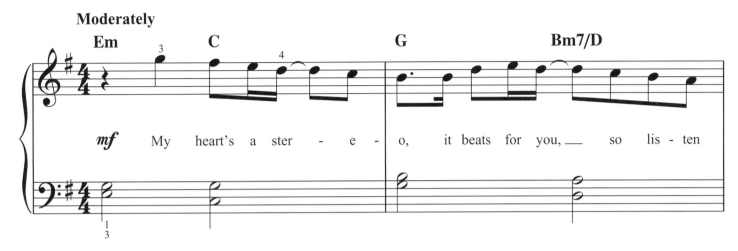

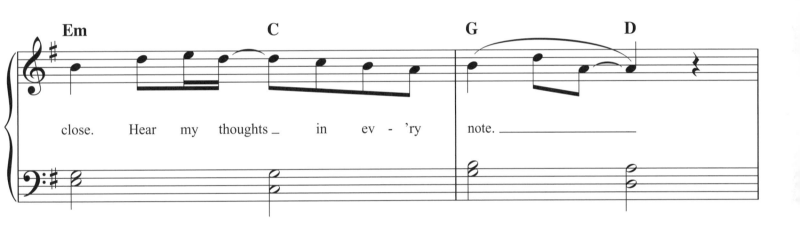

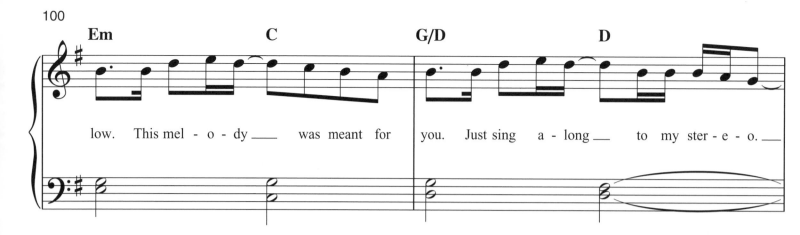

low. This mel - o - dy ___ was meant for you. Just sing a - long ___ to my ster - e - o. ___

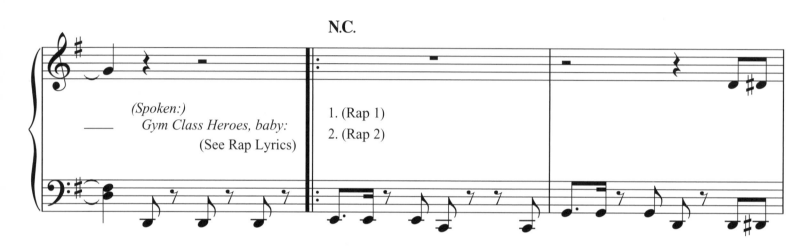

(Spoken:)
___ *Gym Class Heroes, baby:*
(See Rap Lyrics)

1. (Rap 1)
2. (Rap 2)

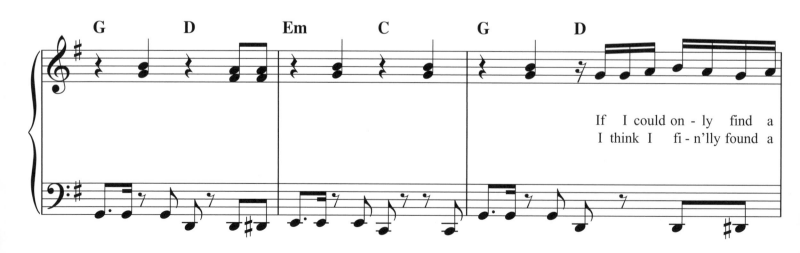

If I could on - ly find a
I think I fi - n'lly found a

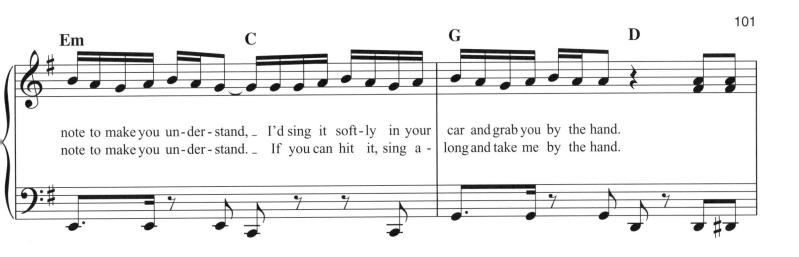

note to make you un-der-stand, _ I'd sing it soft-ly in your car and grab you by the hand.
note to make you un-der-stand. _ If you can hit it, sing a - long and take me by the hand.

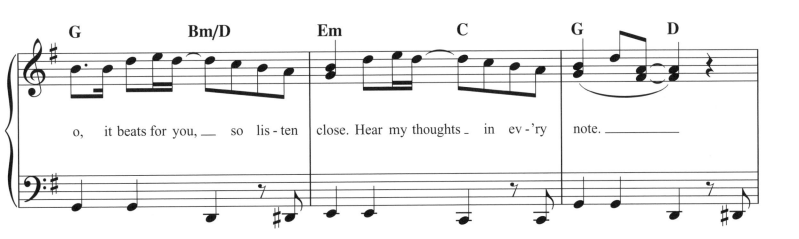

My heart's a ster - e -

o, it beats for you, __ so lis-ten close. Hear my thoughts _ in ev -'ry note. _____

Make me your ra - di - o, and turn me up ___ when you feel low. This mel-o-dy ___ was meant for

you. Just sing a-long __ to my ster-e-o. Oh, oh, __ oh, oh, oh, __ oh.

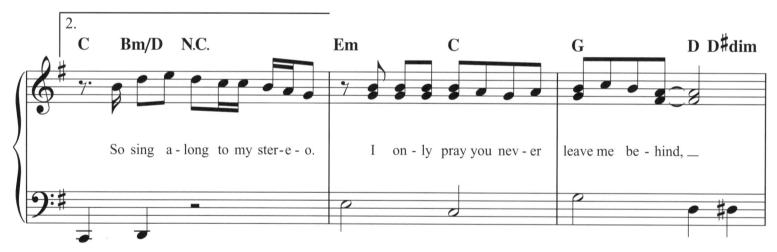

Oh, oh, __ oh, just sing a-long to my ster-e-o. __

So sing a-long to my ster-e-o. I on-ly pray you nev-er leave me be-hind, __

be-cause good mu-sic can be so hard to find. __ I take your head and hold it

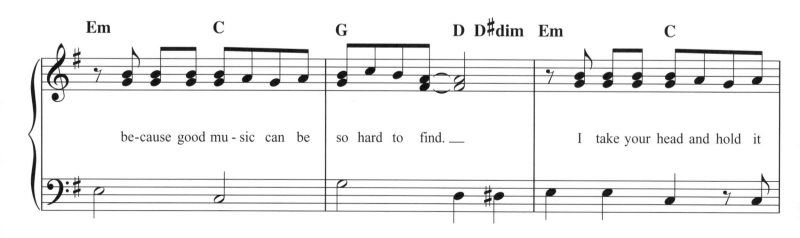

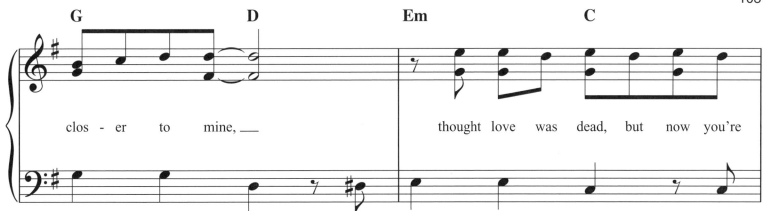

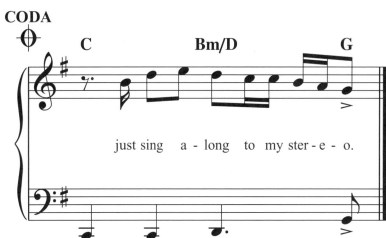

Additional Lyrics

Rap 1: If I was just another dusty record on the shelf,
   Would you blow me off and play me like ev'rybody else?
   If I asked you to scratch my back, could you manage that?
   Like it real, check it, Travie, I can handle that.
   Furthermore, I apologize for any skipping tracks.
   It's just the last girl that played me left a couple cracks.
   I used to, used to, used to, used to, now I'm over that.
   'Cause holding grudges over love is ancient artifacts.

   Just keep it stuck inside your head, like your fav'rite tune,
   And know my heart's a stereo that only plays for you.

Rap 2: If I was an old school fifty-pound boom-box,
   Would you hold me on your shoulder wherever you walk?
   Would you turn my volume up in front of the cops,
   And crank it higher ev'ry time they told you to stop?
   And all I ask is that you don't get mad at me
   When you have to purchase mad "D" batteries.
   Appreciate ev'ry mix-tape your friends make.
   You never know, we come and go like on the interstate.

   Just keep me stuck inside your head, like your fav'rite tune.
   You know my heart's a stereo that only plays for you.

SHAKE IT OFF

Words and Music by TAYLOR SWIFT,
MAX MARTIN and SHELLBACK

at least, that's what peo - ple say, ____ mm, mm. That's what peo - ple
And that's what they don't know, ____ mm, mm. That's what they don't

Am

say, ____ mm, mm. But I keep cruis - ing;
know, ____ mm, mm. But I keep cruis - ing;

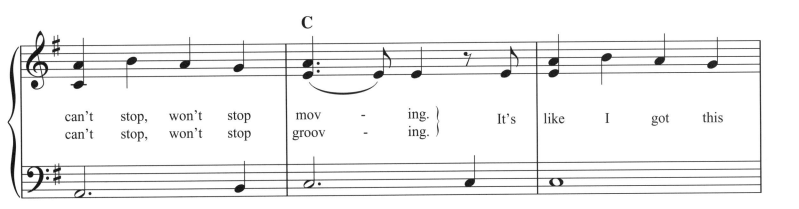

C

can't stop, won't stop mov - ing. It's like I got this
can't stop, won't stop groov - ing.

G

mu - sic in my mind say - ing, "It's gon - na be al - right." ____

fake, fake, fake, ba - by. I'm just gon - na shake, shake, shake, shake, shake; __ I

shake it off, I shake it off. I nev - er miss a off. (Ooh, __ ooh!) I

shake it off, I shake it off. I, I, I shake it off, I shake it

off. I, I, I shake it off, I shake it off. I, I, I

N.C.

shake it off, I shake it off. (Ooh, __ ooh!)

1. *Spoken: (See additional lyrics)*
2. Rap: *(See additional lyrics)*

D.S. al Coda

CODA

G

Rap ends Yeah, __ oh. _____ 'Cause the

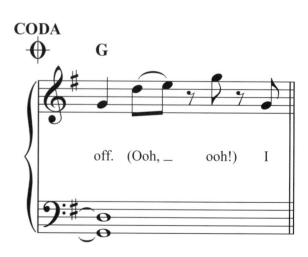

off. (Ooh, __ ooh!) I

Additional Lyrics

Spoken: Hey, hey, hey! Just think: While you've been getting
Down and out about the liars and the dirty, dirty
Cheats of the world, you could've been getting down to
This. Sick. Beat!

Rap: My ex-man brought his new girlfriend.
She's like, "Oh, my god!" But I'm just gonna shake.
And to the fella over there with the hella good hair,
Won't you come on over, baby? We can shake, shake, shake.

A SKY FULL OF STARS

Words and Music by GUY BERRYMAN,
JON BUCKLAND, WILL CHAMPION,
CHRIS MARTIN and TIM BERGLING

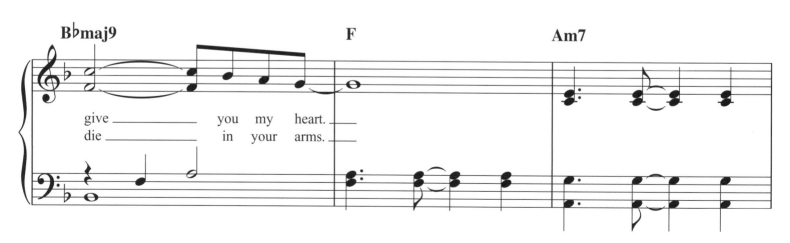

'Cause you're a sky, _____ 'cause you're a sky _____ full of stars.
'Cause you get light - er the more _____ it gets dark. _____

'Cause you light _____ up the path. _____
I'm gon - na give _____ you my heart. _____

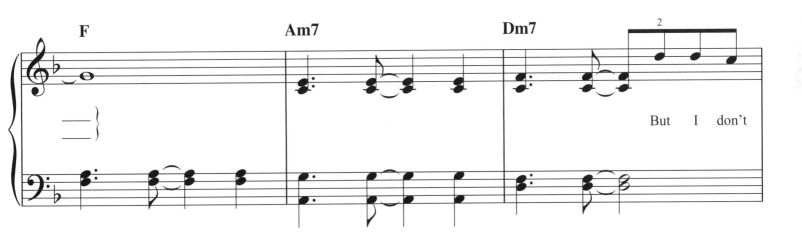

But I don't

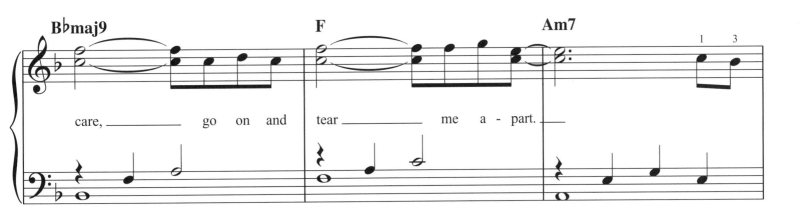

care, _____ go on and tear _____ me a - part. _____

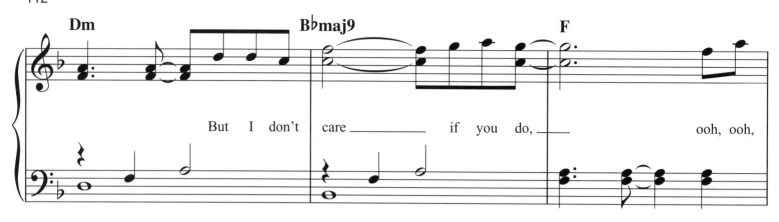

But I don't care _____ if you do, _____ ooh, ooh,

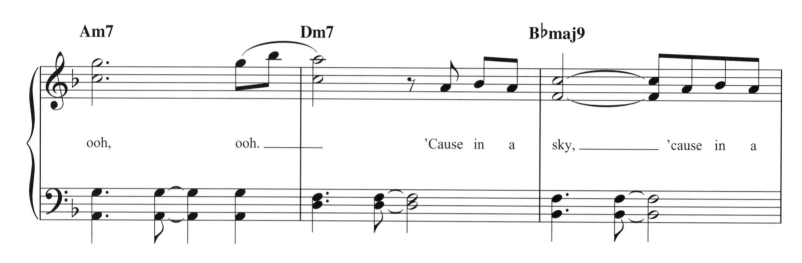

ooh, _____ ooh. _____ 'Cause in a sky, _____ 'cause in a

sky _____ full of stars, _____ I think I {saw / see} you. _____

To Coda ⊕

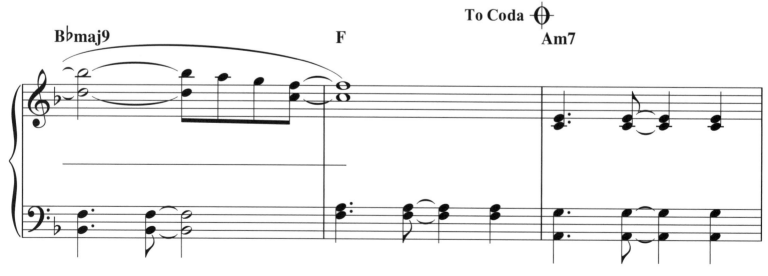

'Cause you're a sky, _____ you're a sky _____

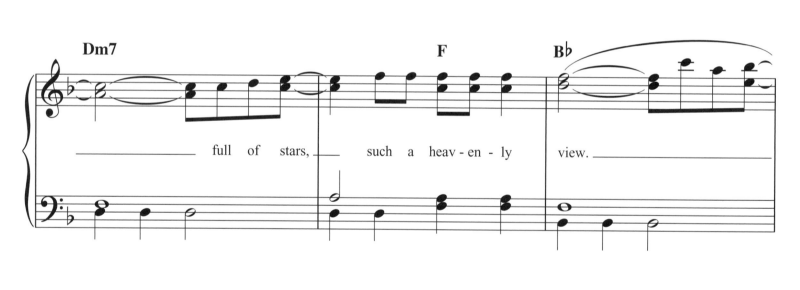

_____ full of stars, ___ such a heav-en-ly view. _____

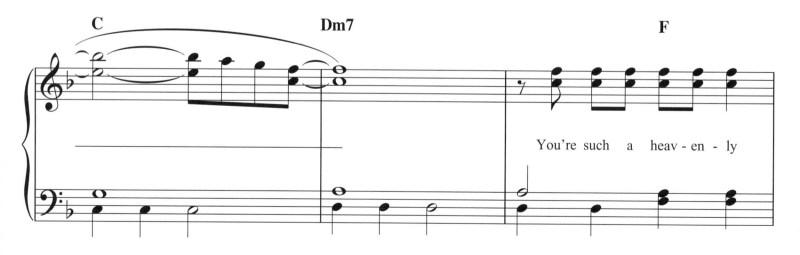

You're such a heav-en-ly

STORY OF MY LIFE

Words and Music by JAMIE SCOTT,
JOHN HENRY RYAN, JULIAN BUNETTA,
HARRY STYLES, LIAM PAYNE,
LOUIS TOMLINSON, NIALL HORAN
and ZAIN MALIK

feel the same a-bout us in her bones.
see a sin-gle light up-on the hill. Al -

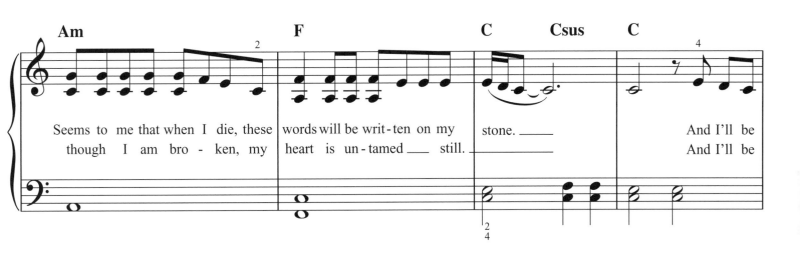

Seems to me that when I die, these words will be writ-ten on my stone. _____ And I'll be
though I am bro-ken, my heart is un-tamed ___ still. _____ And I'll be

gone, gone to-night. ___ The ground be-neath my feet is o - pen wide, ___ the way that I've been
gone, gone to-night. ___ The fire be-neath my feet is burn - in' bright, ___ the way that I've been

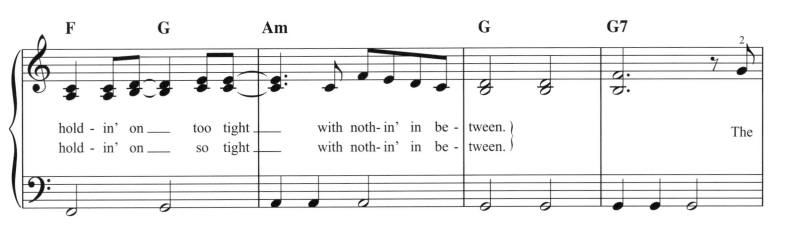

hold - in' on ___ too tight ___ with noth-in' in be - tween.
hold - in' on ___ so tight ___ with noth-in' in be - tween.   The

sto - ry of my life. I take her home.__ I drive all night__ to keep her warm ____ and

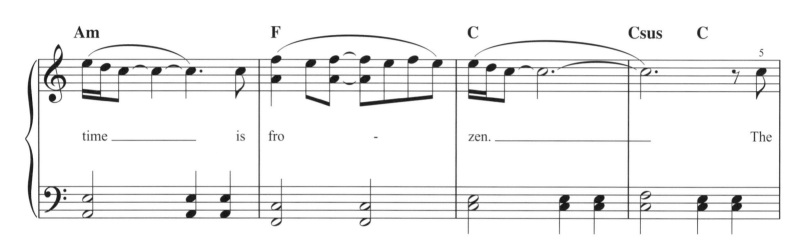

time _____ is fro - zen._____ The

sto - ry of my life. I give her hope.__ I spend her love __ un - til she's broke ____ in -

side. _____ The sto - ry of my life. _____

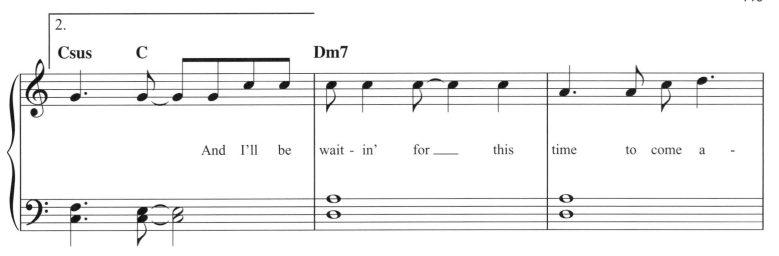

And I'll be wait-in' for ___ this time to come a-

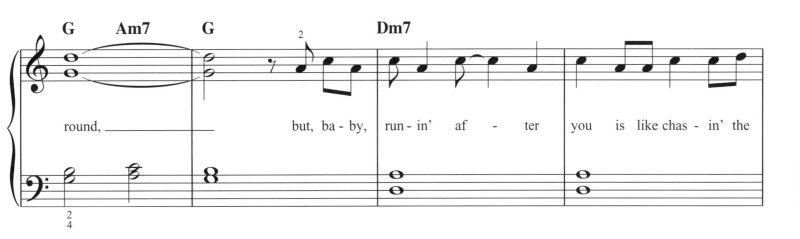

round, ___ but, ba-by, run-in' af - ter you is like chas - in' the

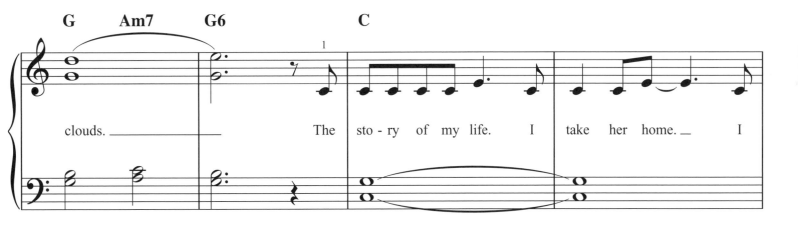

clouds. ___ The sto-ry of my life. I take her home. __ I

drive all night ___ to keep her warm. ___ And time ___ is

STRONGER
(What Doesn't Kill You)

Words and Music by GREG KURSTIN,
ALEXANDRA TAMPOSI, DAVID GAMSON
and JORGEN ELOFSSON

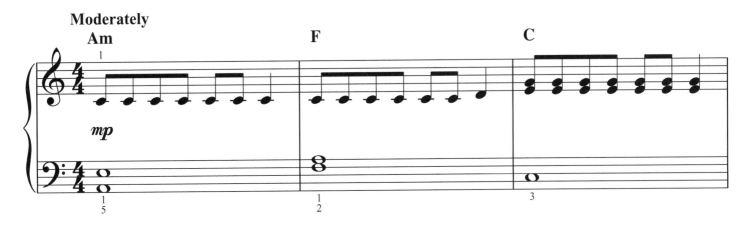

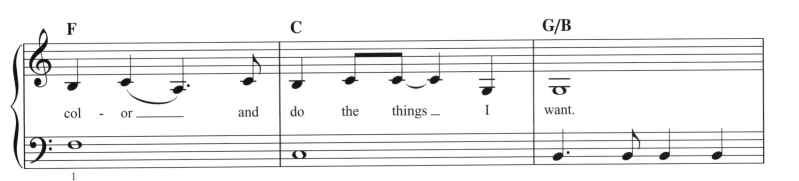

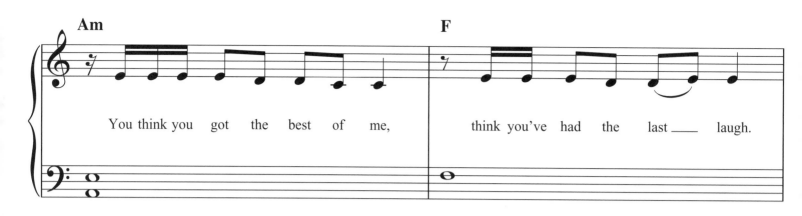

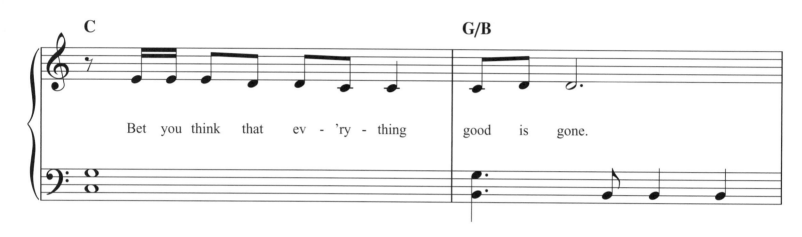

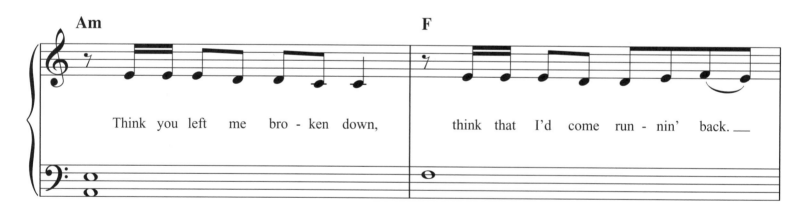

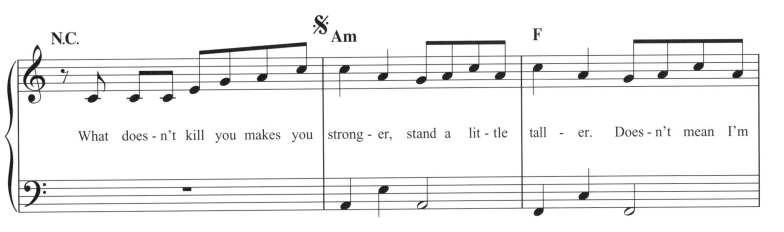

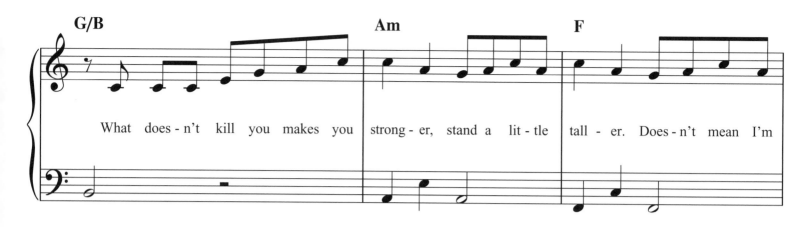

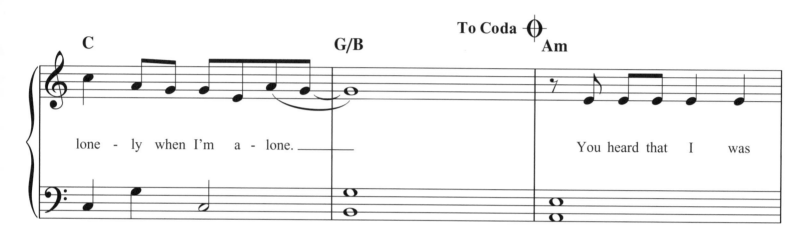

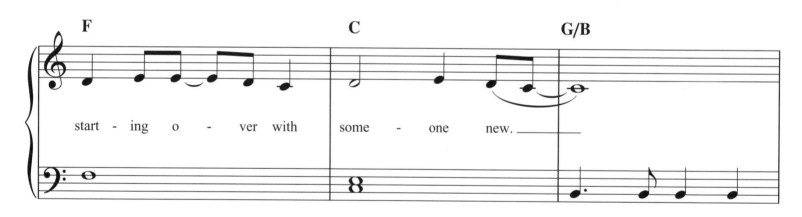

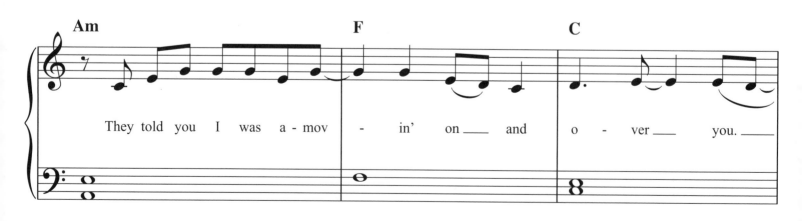

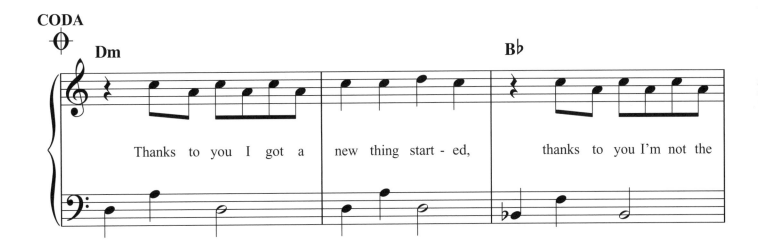

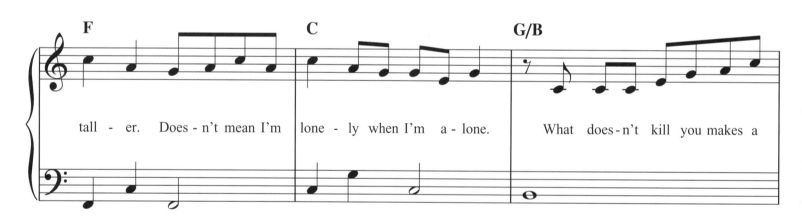

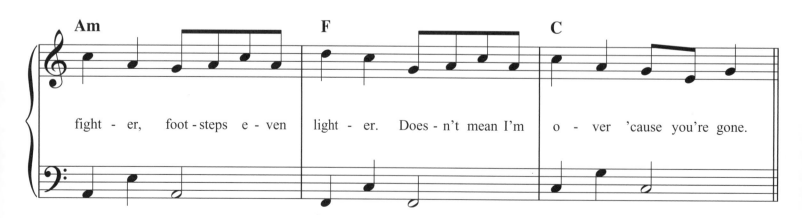

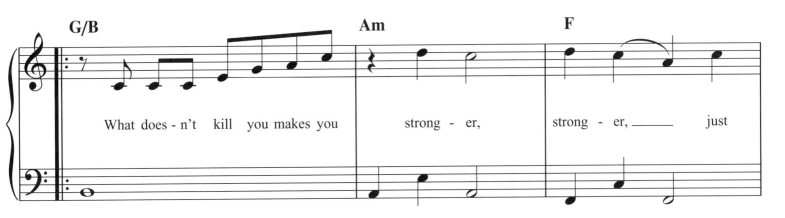

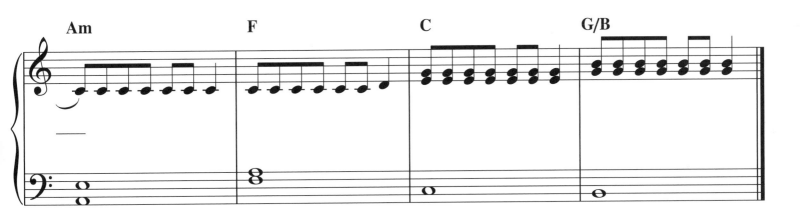

SUPERHEROES

Words and Music by DANNY O'DONOGHUE,
MARK SHEEHAN and JAMES BARRY

life, she has seen all the mean-er side ___ of mean. They took a-

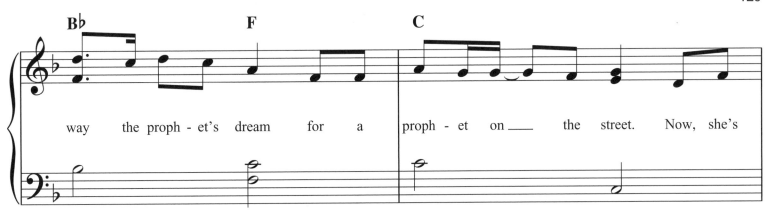

way the proph-et's dream for a proph-et on ___ the street. Now, she's

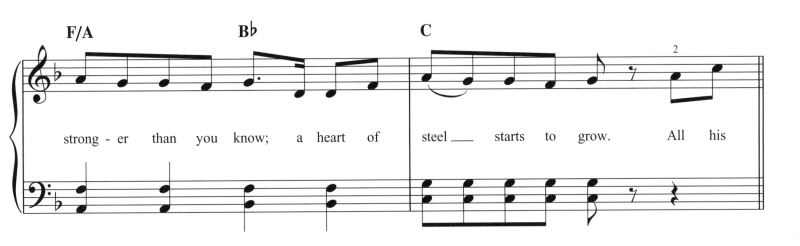

strong-er than you know; a heart of steel ___ starts to grow. All his

life he's been told he'll be noth-ing when ___ he's old. All the
hurt, all the lies, all the tears ___ that ___ they cry; when the

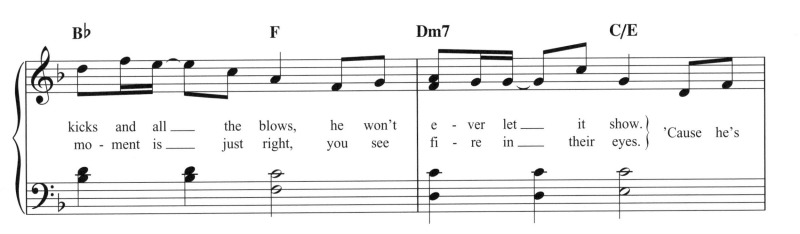

kicks and all ___ the blows, he won't e - ver let ___ it show.   'Cause he's
mo - ment is ___ just right, you see fi - re in ___ their eyes.

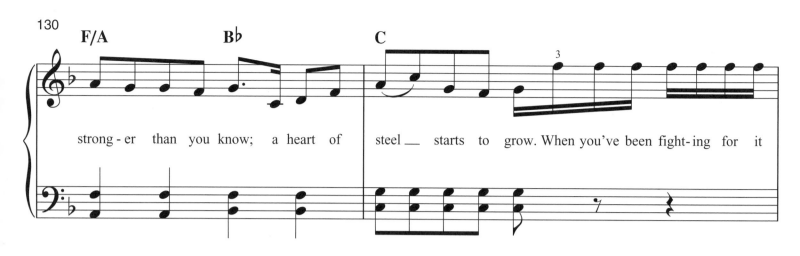

strong - er than you know; a heart of steel ___ starts to grow. When you've been fight - ing for it

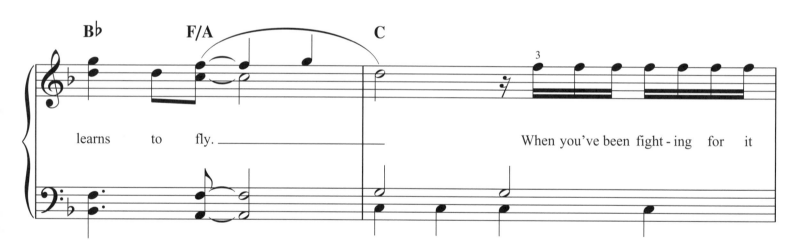

all your life, ___ you've been strug - gl - ing to make things right, ___ that's how a su - per - he - ro

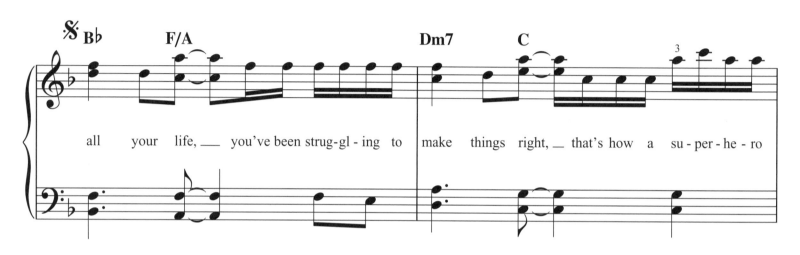

learns to fly. _____ When you've been fight - ing for it

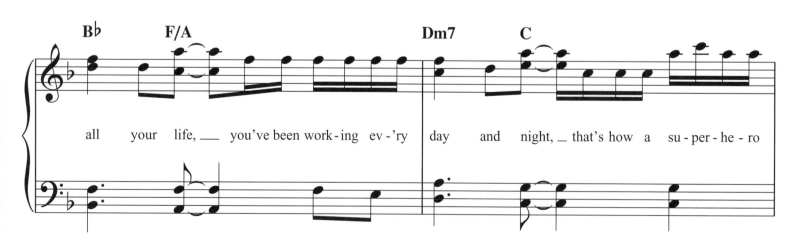

all your life, ___ you've been work - ing ev - 'ry day and night, ___ that's how a su - per - he - ro

ex - plode, ex - plode, ex - plode. When you've been fight - ing for it

When you've been fight-ing for it all your life, __ you've been strug-gl-ling to

make things right, __ that's how a su - per - he - ro learns to fly. __

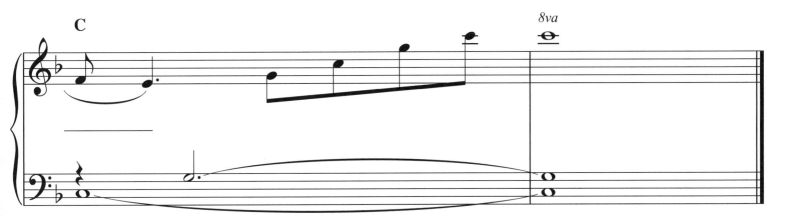

WHAT DO I KNOW?

Words and Music by ED SHEERAN,
FOY VANCE and JOHNNY McDAID

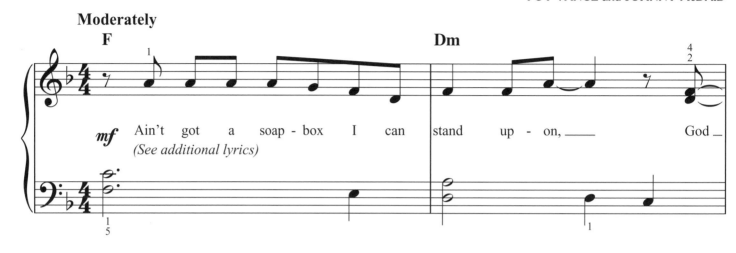

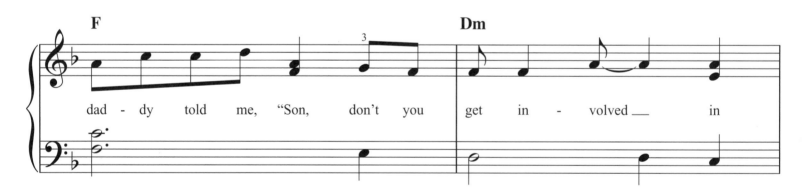

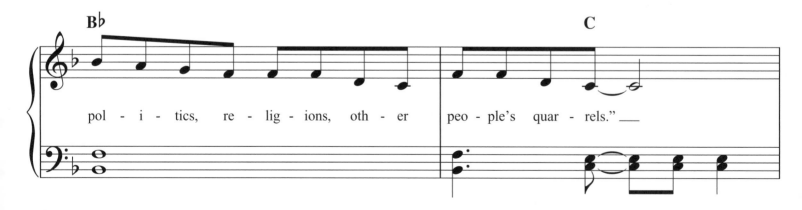

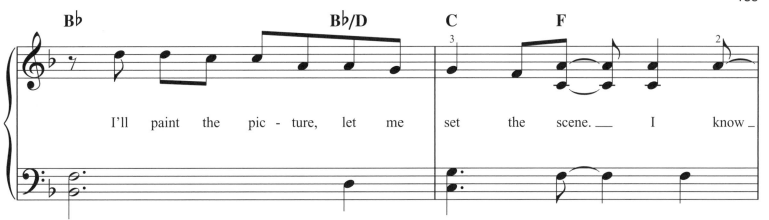

I'll paint the pic - ture, let me set the scene.___ I know___

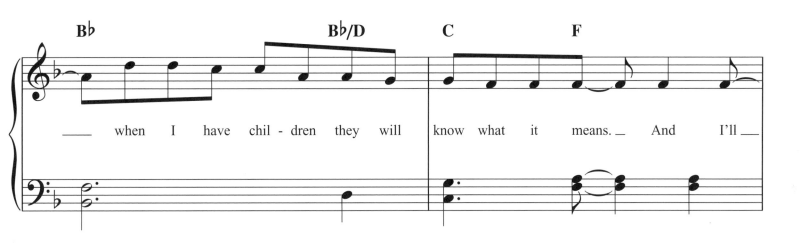

___ when I have chil - dren they will know what it means.___ And I'll___

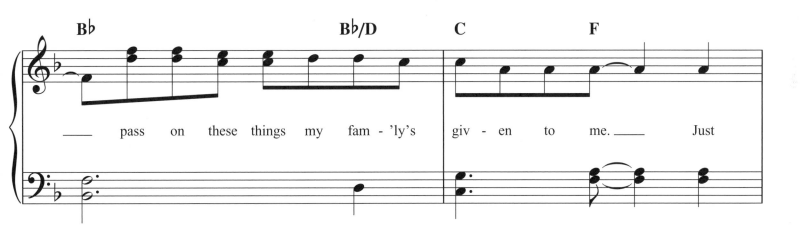

___ pass on these things my fam - 'ly's giv - en to me.___ Just

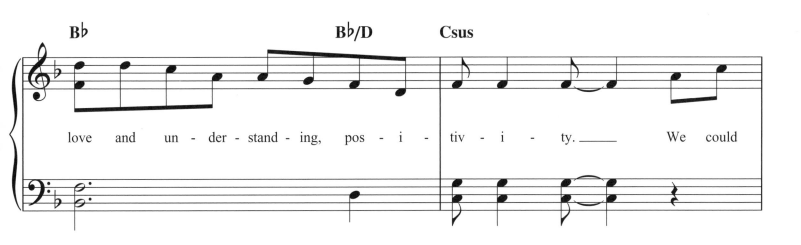

love and un - der - stand - ing, pos - i - tiv - i - ty.___ We could

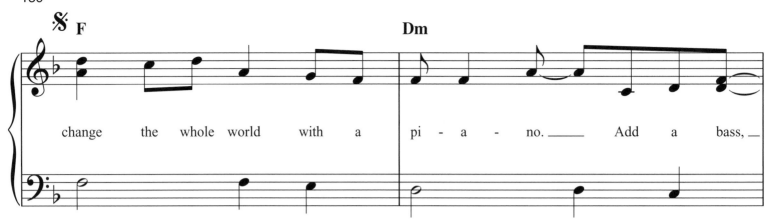

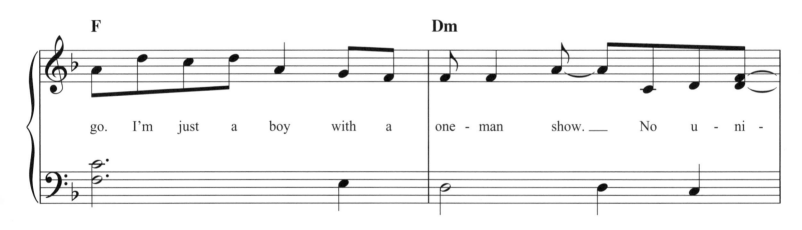

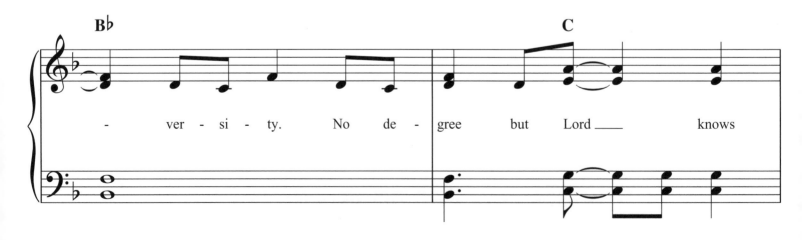

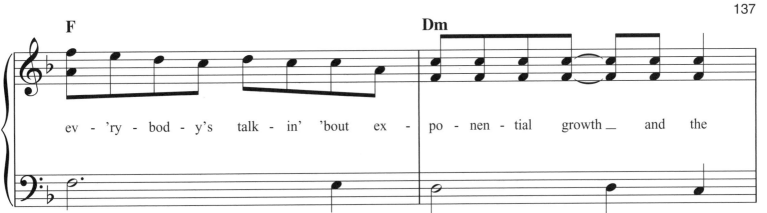

ev - ’ry - bod - y’s talk - in’ ’bout ex - po - nen - tial growth __ and the

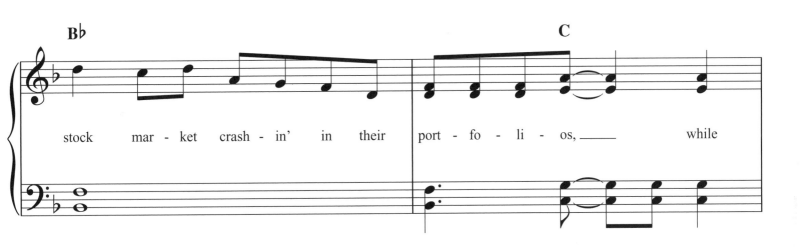

stock mar - ket crash - in’ in their port - fo - li - os, _____ while

I’ll be sit - tin’ here with a song that I wrote. __ Sing,

love can change the world in a mo - ment, but what do I _____ know?

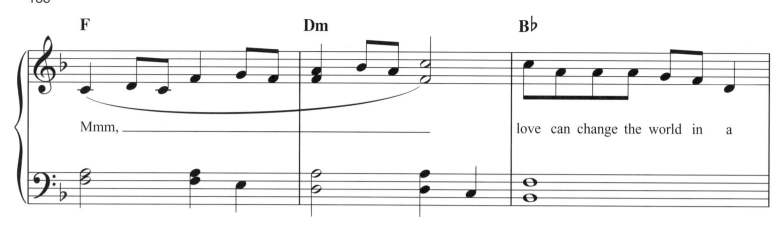

Mmm, _____ love can change the world in a

mo-ment, but what do I ___ know? Mmm, _____

love can change the world in a mo-ment. The mo-ment.

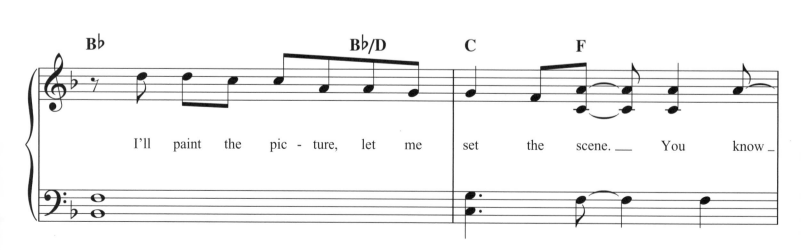

I'll paint the pic-ture, let me set the scene. ___ You know _

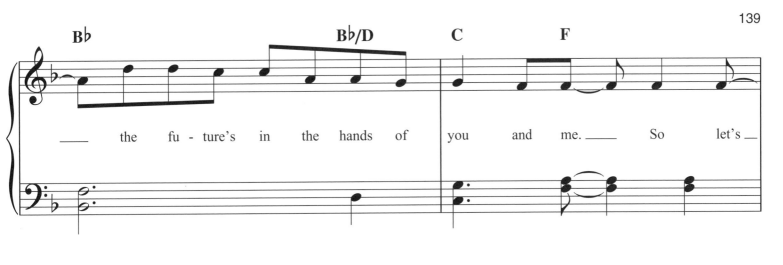

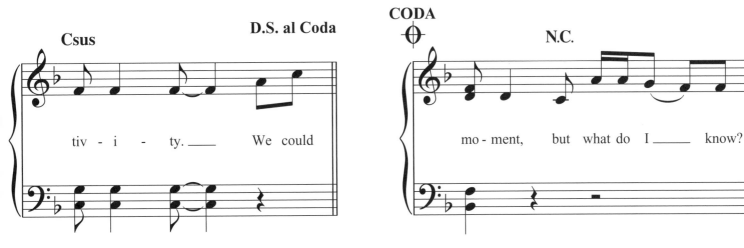

Additional Lyrics

The revolution's comin', it's a minute away.
I saw people marching in the streets today.
You know we are made up of love and hate,
But both of them are balanced on a razor blade.
I'll paint the picture, let me set the scene.
I know I'm all for people followin' their dreams.
Just remember life is more than fittin' in your dreams.
It's love and understanding, positivity.

WHAT MAKES YOU BEAUTIFUL

Words and Music by SAVAN KOTECHA,
RAMI YACOUB and CARL FALK

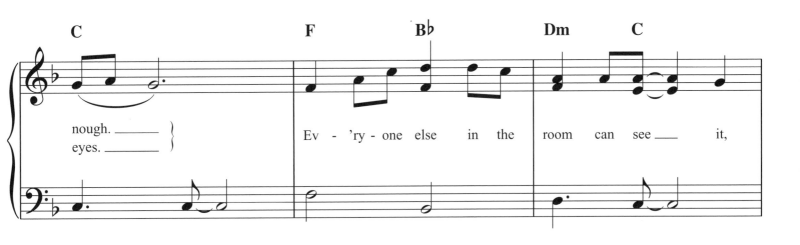

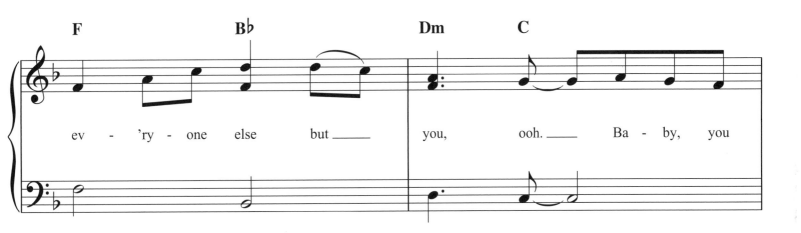

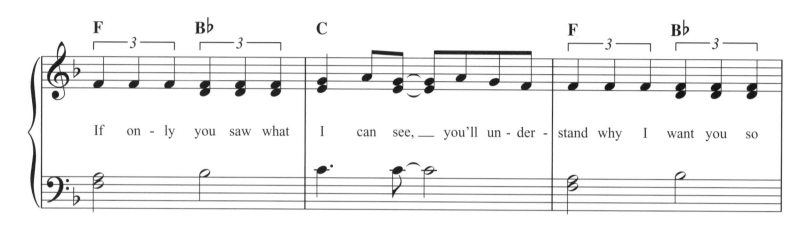

light up my world like no - bod - y else. ___ The way that

you flip your hair gets me o - ver - whelmed. ___ But when you smile at the ground, it ain't

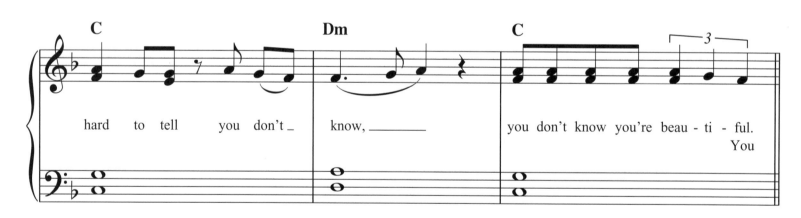

hard to tell you don't ___ know, ___ you don't know you're beau - ti - ful.
You

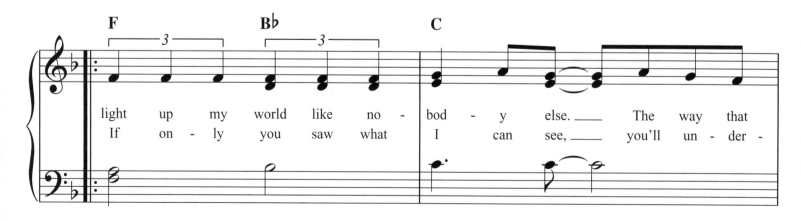

light up my world like no - bod - y else. ___ The way that
If on - ly you saw what I can see, ___ you'll un - der -

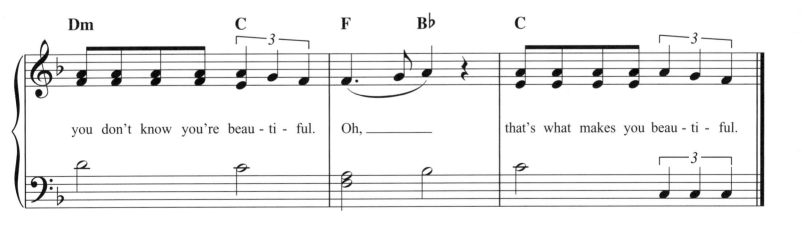

TRY

Words and Music by COLBIE CAILLAT,
JASON REEVES, ANTONIO DIXON
and KENNETH EDMONDS

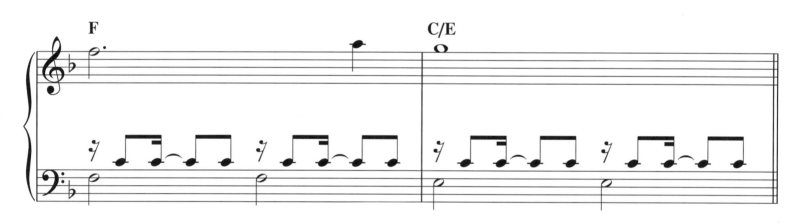

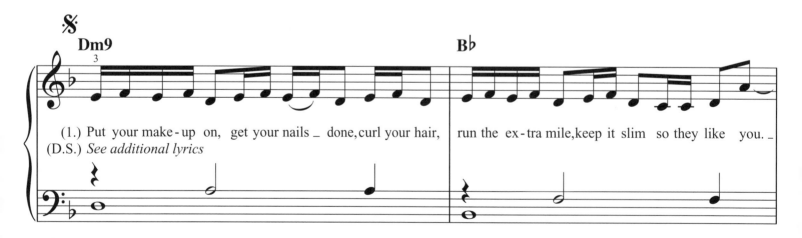

(1.) Put your make-up on, get your nails done, curl your hair, run the ex-tra mile, keep it slim so they like you.

(D.S.) *See additional lyrics*

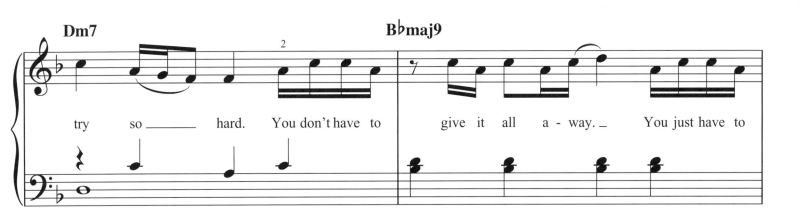

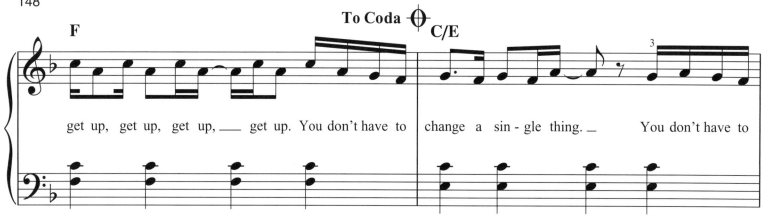

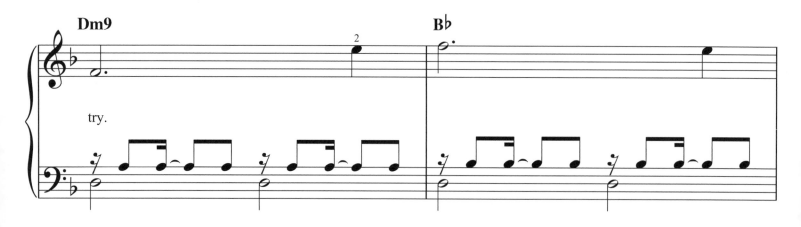

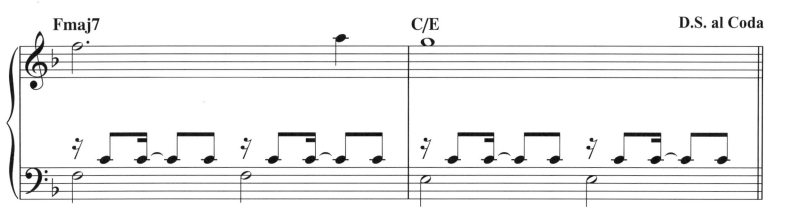

D.S. al Coda

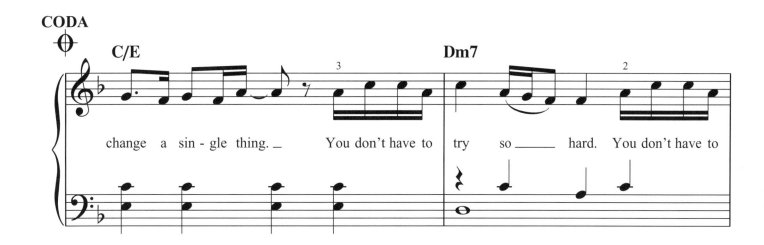

change a sin - gle thing. __ You don't have to try so __ hard. You don't have to

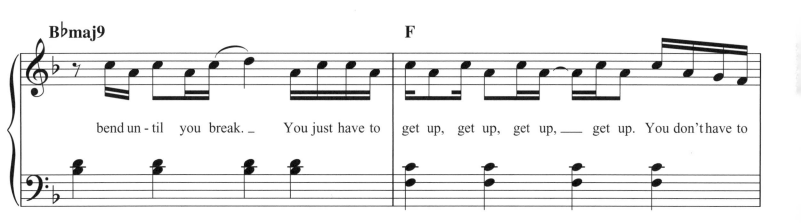

bend un - til you break. __ You just have to get up, get up, get up, __ get up. You don't have to

change a sin - gle thing. __ You don't have to try, try, try, try, __ I, I. You don't have to

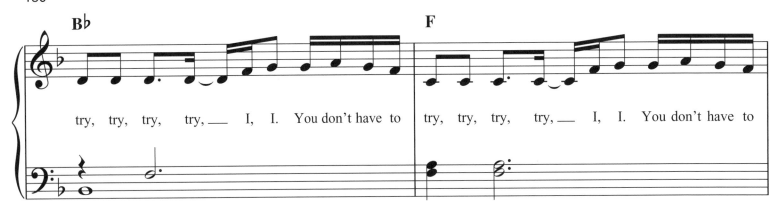

B♭

try, try, try, try, __ I, I. You don't have to

F

try, try, try, try, __ I, I. You don't have to

C/E

try.   No, you don't have to

Dm

try, try, try, try, __ I, I. You don't have to

B♭

try, try, try, try, __ I, I. You don't have to

F

try, try, try, try, __ I, I. You don't have to

C/E

try.   You ____ don't have to

Dm7

try. _____

B♭

Oo, _____

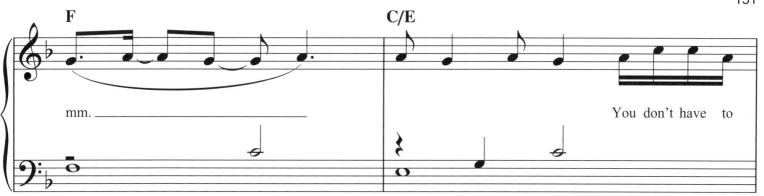

F   **C/E**

mm. _____

You don't have to

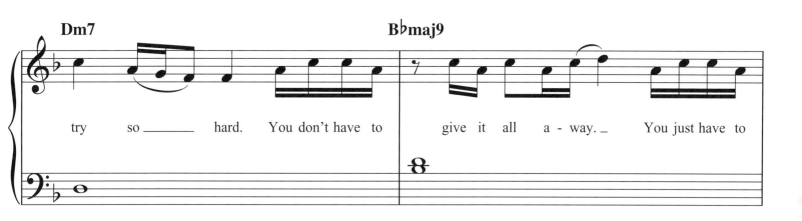

Dm7   **B♭maj9**

try so _____ hard. You don't have to give it all a - way. _____ You just have to

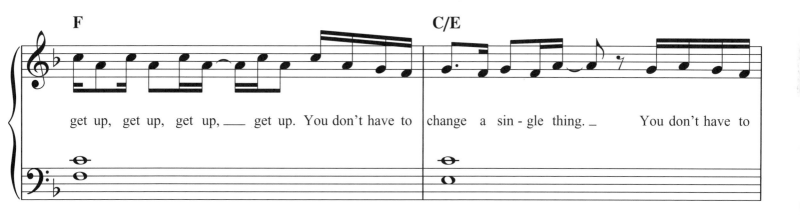

F   **C/E**

get up, get up, get up, _____ get up. You don't have to change a sin - gle thing. _____ You don't have to

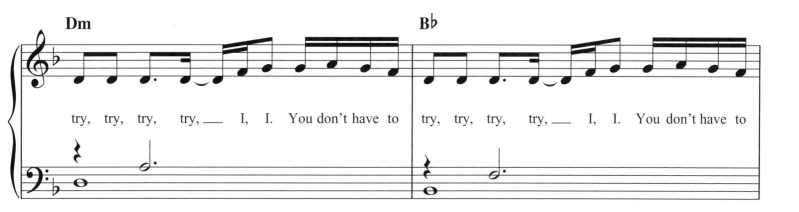

Dm   **B♭**

try, try, try, try, _____ I, I. You don't have to try, try, try, try, _____ I, I. You don't have to

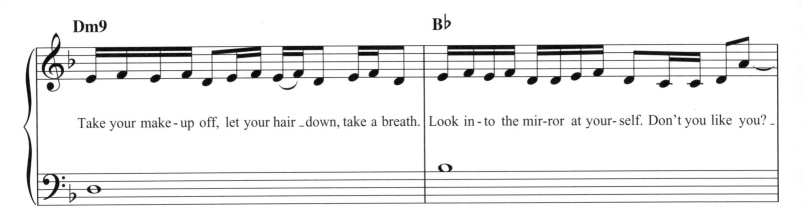

try.   You don't have to try.

Take your make-up off, let your hair down, take a breath.   Look in-to the mir-ror at your-self. Don't you like you?

'Cause I like you.

Additional Lyrics

Get your shoppin' on at the mall. Max your credit cards.
You don't have to choose, buy it all so they like you.
Do they like you?
Wait a second, should you care what they think of you?
When you're all alone by yourself, do you like you?
Do you like you?